H to survive counsellor tr...ng

TW

How to survive counsellor training

An A–Z Guide

Rowan Bayne

Professor of Psychology and Counselling,
School of Psychology,
University of East London, UK

Gordon Jinks

Principal Lecturer in Counselling and Psychotherapy,
University of East London, UK

First published 2010 by
PALGRAVE MACMILLAN

Palgrave Macmillan in the UK is an imprint of Macmillan Publishers Limited, registered in England, company number 785998, of Houndmills, Basingstoke, Hampshire RG21 6XS.

Palgrave Macmillan in the US is a division of St Martin's Press LLC, 175 Fifth Avenue, New York, NY 10010.

Palgrave Macmillan is the global academic imprint of the above companies and has companies and representatives throughout the world.

Palgrave® and Macmillan® are registered trademarks in the United States, the United Kingdom, Europe and other countries

ISBN 978-0-230-21712-6

This book is printed on paper suitable for recycling and made from fully managed and sustained forest sources. Logging, pulping and manufacturing processes are expected to conform to the environmental regulations of the country of origin.

A catalogue record for this book is available from the British Library.

A catalog record for this book is available from the Library of Congress

Contents

Acknowledgements

A very warm thank you to Tracy Boakes and Katherine Bayne for being positive, lively and calm; to Debra Jinks for support, encouragement and some good ideas; to Catherine Gray for her stimulating and perceptive editing; to Caroline Richards for skilful copy-editing; and to our students for being variously puzzled, warm, challenging, surprising and fun.

Introduction

Training to be a counsellor or psychotherapist can be an intense and demanding experience, emotionally and intellectually. Experience and what research is available suggest that it's also generally positive and fulfilling but that there is scope for improvement. In this book, therefore, we review those aspects of training which trainees tend to find stressful or puzzling and which we think being clearer about will contribute to surviving – and enjoying – a course.

Our aims are to reduce anxiety, to correct misinformation, to help and encourage you to take care of yourself and pay attention to your experience, to inform your choices and suggest possible actions and strategies. We therefore suggest the rationales behind some aspects of training, offer some hints about how to get the most out of the experience, warn you about some of the challenges you might face, suggest strategies for coping with them, and overall hope to enable you to maximise the gains and manage the costs involved more effectively.

We have written the book for students taking counselling, psychotherapy and coaching courses. It should also be helpful to people who are deciding whether or not to apply for counsellor training.

Training institutions

At present, counsellor training is available at a wide range of institutions, from private training organisations, through colleges and further education and into the higher education sector (both at undergraduate and postgraduate level), and there is wide variation in format, depending on the type of institution, the academic level and model or models of counselling central to a course, and the training, interests and personalities of the tutors.

Most of this book applies to counsellor training generally, but a few sections – for example those which give some guidance on how to address assessment criteria as they are likely to be presented in a higher education setting – might not be directly relevant to the course you are taking. Similarly, although this book's main reference points are British, we hope its ideas and guidance will be helpful to readers in other countries too.

At the time of writing, the future direction of counsellor training in the UK is unclear in some ways. The introduction of statutory regulation for the profession under the auspices of the Health Professions Council (HPC) is due to be implemented in 2011. Exactly how this will affect training remains to be seen, but it seems likely that the issue of HPC approval, so that those successfully completing the course are able to gain entry to the professional register, will come to the fore. This could, in the long term, mean that counsellor training moves in the direction of higher education, or at least higher education validation of courses, as this is the norm for other professions regulated by the HPC.

Core elements of training

As noted above, counsellor training courses vary, and there is no standard format. However, some or all of the following are likely to be present on many courses:

▸ Lecture sessions where information about theories, models, qualities, skills, processes, client issues, professional and ethical issues etc. is presented or discussed.

▸ Workshop sessions where material such as the above is worked with through practical activities, applications are considered, and students are able to deepen their understanding and reflect on what it means and how it can be useful.

▸ Experiential activities (experiential group, personal development group etc.), where the focus is on engaging with yourself and others, participating in reflection and learning from your personal experience of what you are doing. Self-awareness and personal development are more important here than learning facts or theories.

▸ Skills training sessions (skills labs, practicum sessions etc.), where you have an opportunity to practise the specific skills you are learning with peers and receive feedback on how you are doing.

▸ Supervision, where you have the opportunity to discuss your work with clients, and other issues pertinent to your development as a counsellor, with an experienced practitioner.

▸ Community meetings, where the experience of being on the course is the primary consideration and the 'community' of those involved (both students and staff) have an opportunity to share their impressions, questions, and indeed the responsibility for their shared experience.

▸ Tutorials, where either one-to-one or in small groups you have the opportunity to discuss particular issues, your progress, assessment tasks etc. with a tutor.

▸ Personal therapy, where you experience directly what it is like to be a client, and have the opportunity to work on those issues which need to be addressed to further your development and enable you to function better both as a counsellor and, hopefully, as a person.

▸ Assessment. In some way, and probably in a variety of ways, you will be required to demonstrate that you have achieved the necessary elements as defined by your course and have reached the standards required.

‣ Personal reflection. Key to all of the above is that you take the time to reflect on what you are experiencing and what you are learning. You need time to integrate information, to consider its application and value, to process your feelings and consider your behaviour, make sense of what you are experiencing, explore the impact that you are having on others (and them on you), evaluate what you are doing, recognise your strengths and resources, acknowledge areas for development, identify aims and goals, and think about how you will achieve them.

The A–Z format of this book

The A–Z format suits both the subject and the way we see the book being used. It allows readers to quickly and easily find ideas, evidence and arguments, and to read further entries on related topics if they wish, following a variety of 'routes'. For example, a reader interested in a rationale for the open circle would go to that entry and might then, through the 'See also' section at the beginning of the entry, go to 'Beginning of each training day', or to 'Self-awareness', and from 'Self-awareness' to 'Co-counselling', 'Journal', 'Personality', 'Motives for being a counsellor', 'Strengths' and so on …

Theory

In this book we generally apply theories rather than describe or discuss them. That is more a role for general textbooks, e.g. Feltham and Horton (2006), Bayne et al. (2008), McLeod (2009). However, we do say something about the rationales for including certain theories in counsellor training, and three theories in particular have entries of their own and are each applied or referred to in several other entries: on assertiveness theory, a theory of loss, and psychological type theory in its Myers–Briggs Type Indicator (MBTI) sense. These are included because we see them as having particular relevance to the central theme of the book – how to survive, get the most out of and enjoy your training.

There is a potentially bewildering, confusing and contradictory range of theory available to counsellors, and the recommended reading at the end of this introduction may help you at least to orientate yourself and supplement or clarify what you learn on your course. We believe, too, that so far no one theory or model can account for the complexity of human experience and behaviour, or indeed for the complexity of the counselling interaction, and that as a result counsellors need to be able to work with a range of (sometimes contradictory) ideas and frameworks.

However, we are also somewhat reassured by the evidence which suggests that theory is relatively unimportant in terms of enabling positive outcomes for clients in counselling (see entry on 'Integrative counselling'). What seems to matter much more is engaging with the client's resources in a positive therapeutic relationship, and working in ways that make sense to them. Most training approaches will at least agree with the general idea (if not necessarily the precise terms) of a relationship based on empathy (understanding, sharing, common frame of reference etc.), acceptance (non-judgemental, unconditional positive regard etc.) and genuineness (congruence, openness, trustworthiness etc.).

The authors

We've been trainers on counselling and interpersonal skills courses for over 50 years between us and with people from a wide variety of jobs and counselling orientations. Our own orientations are broadly similar: an integration of the person-centred 'core qualities' with techniques from a variety of approaches, for example CBT, narrative counselling, co-counselling, existential therapy and Gestalt therapy.

We like the following books and recommend that you have a look at them, and also, first, at the entry in this book on 'Reading lists' and ways of approaching them.

Windy Dryden, *Counselling in a Nutshell* (Sage, 1990).
> A clear, informal and authoritative introduction, written for those beginning counsellor training or those who wish to know more about what counsellors do.

Rowan Bayne, Gordon Jinks, Patrizia Collard and Ian Horton, *The Counsellor's Handbook. A Practical A–Z Guide to Integrative Counselling and Psychotherapy*, 3rd edition (Nelson Thornes, 2008).
> Brief entries on about 150 everyday aspects of counselling, e.g. beginnings, boundaries, congruence, common factors, difficult clients, emotions, empathy, multiculturalism, paraphrasing, sexual attraction, silence, stress, supervision, etc.

Two more detailed general texts are:

Colin Feltham and Ian Horton (eds), *The Sage Handbook of Counselling and Psychotherapy*, 2nd edition (Sage, 2006).

John McLeod, *An Introduction to Counselling*, 4th edition (Oxford University Press, 2009).

Some more specialised books:

Mark A. Hubble, Barry L. Duncan and Scott D. Miller (eds), *The Heart and Soul of Change: What Works in Therapy* (American Psychological Association, 1999).

Provides a coherent and inspiring synthesis of the 'common factors' research and its implications for practice.

Dave Mearns and Brian Thorne, *Person-Centred Counselling in Action*, 3rd edition (Sage, 2007).

See particularly the chapters on empathy, congruence and 'unconditional positive regard'. Even when your course's approach to counselling is not person-centred, the qualities identified by Carl Rogers are commonly seen as important to understanding the therapeutic relationship.

Irvin D. Yalom, *Love's Executioner and Other Tales of Psychotherapy* (Penguin, 1989).

Vivid discussions of counselling with ten clients.

Tim Bond, *Standards and Ethics for Counselling in Action*, 3rd edition (Sage, 2009).

Discusses ethical dilemmas, e.g. suicidal clients, and ethical principles and decision making.

a

age and applying for counsellor training

> ▷ application forms, assertiveness, critical thinking, experience, rejection, selection, strengths

Despite recent legislation, age is a fixed criterion for entry to some counselling courses: applications from people who are less than 26 or more than 65, for example, are rejected automatically. This criterion confuses chronological age with what may be called real age. At the lower age limit, it confuses years lived with maturity and self-awareness; age in years doesn't tell us much about adults' abilities in general, let alone about a particular adult.

It may be worth arguing that you are an exception if you are unusually young or old to apply for counsellor training (and the average age is probably about 35 years with a typical range of, say, 26 to 55), or, of course, if you don't meet the age criterion for a course you want to apply for. A stated age limit is more likely at the lower end, but the higher end may in practice be a barrier too. Acknowledge your age and make a reasoned case, positively stated, with some detailed examples, showing how you think you meet the other selection criteria. (See particularly the entries on Application forms, Experience and Strengths.)

angry, feeling

> ▷ assertiveness, journal, self-awareness, trust

Anger is an emotion which is often linked to a sense of injustice or threat. It is likely that you will have felt angry yourself and experienced others being angry in a range of situations. You may also encounter it during your counsellor training or in work with clients.

Anger is natural and can be both healthy and useful in increasing determination and mobilising resources to address injustice. However, if uncontrolled or managed ineffectively it can also have negative consequences, reducing your ability to process information effectively and control behaviour. Anger can occur as a relatively quick emotional response when something happens that seems unfair or threatening, or it can develop as a more sustained emotional state in response to ongoing perceived injustice. Individuals vary in terms of what triggers anger, how it is experienced and how it is expressed (or not). Stress and anxiety can also affect the way anger is triggered and expressed.

As a counsellor, it is important that you are able to allow clients to experience and express anger because it may be an important part of their story, or a factor in the problems they wish to deal with. Anger can feature in clients' problems in a range of ways, from being an emotion which they have repressed, attempted to deny or are afraid of in others, to being experienced powerfully and frequently leading to inappropriate aggression, violence or intimidation. Counsellors who are themselves afraid of or uncomfortable with anger may discourage clients from getting in touch with their feelings or expressing them, and may be tempted to collude with clients to avoid becoming a target for anger.

Anger is most likely to be constructive rather than destructive if it is recognised, reflected on, and expressed appropriately by the person who feels it, avoiding direct aggression (or violence), indirect aggression (such as withdrawal or isolation), or resentment. Anger and aggression are linked but they are not the same thing, and expression of anger in a non-aggressive way can lead to exploration of the perceived causes or triggers, discussion of any injustice or unfairness which is felt, and, hopefully, negotiation and resolution.

It is likely that your counselling training will at times generate circumstances in which either you feel angry (with peers, tutors, clients or yourself) or someone else on the course does. The level of trust in the course group will hopefully develop enough (see entry on Trust) for there to be opportunities to practise feeling, expressing and exploring anger in constructive ways, or facilitating others in doing so.

Some prompts for reflecting on anger:

- Try to take some time (however brief) to reflect on what else you are feeling.
- What exactly are you experiencing (feelings, thoughts, physically)?
- What do you see as the cause of your anger?
- Who are you angry with?
- What perceived threats, unfairness or injustice are you responding to?
- What else is going on in your life right now that might be contributing to your feelings?
- What past experiences might be shaping your responses?
- Are these feelings familiar, part of a pattern?
- How much do you know about what any other people involved might feel?
- How could this be resolved satisfactorily? What do you actually want?
- How reasonable and realistic is that?
- How might a 'win–win' outcome be achieved?

For discussions of anger and anger management, see Williams and Scott (2006) and the website of the British Association of Anger Management.

application forms

▷ assertiveness, critical thinking, experience, qualifications, references (for applications), selection, strengths

Some people attracted to counsellor training – probably most – find the idea of selling themselves unappealing. It may help to think of completing an application form not as selling yourself or 'making a pitch' but as opening a negotiation in which you describe yourself honestly and the selectors describe themselves and their course honestly.

Your honesty here, as in the counselling skill of self-disclosure, doesn't mean an unflinching bluntness or total openness. It means selecting the most relevant information (evidence) from your experience, beliefs and other knowledge about yourself, and then using other skills and qualities relevant to counselling and counsellor training – critical thinking, self-awareness – to present it with impact. It also means investigating the other people in the negotiation and seeking to be clear about their needs and values.

In our view, the main errors perpetrated in the most important section of the standard application form, the 'personal statement', are (1) lack of selection of material (conciseness is good); (2) lack of impact (some sense of language is vital); (3) lack of structure (e.g. a stream of consciousness approach); and (4) lack of specificity or concreteness (give a specific example or two for general claims or briefly explain something that may be interpreted negatively).

Take the final suggestion above, for example, and consider an applicant who has had more jobs than most people. How do *you* interpret this fact? (As a critical thinking exercise, you might at this point like to actually think of as many interpretations as you can.) And second, if it were your application, how would you present this aspect of your experience?

Some interpretations of numerous changes of job are:

- no staying power (this may be the most common interpretation, rightly or wrongly);
- range of experience and is now ready for a more committed approach;
- a lot of these jobs may have been temporary;
- such an effective worker that she's been headhunted or promoted often;
- antagonises employers for some reason and is encouraged to move on;
- has been experimenting and gradually developing a sense of what is right for him by discovering what isn't right;
- unrealistic expectations of work;
- bad luck.

A trained interviewer will probably try to find out which of these explanations, or a variation, is most true, but you can save the interviewer some work and, crucially, make being offered an interview more likely, if you're appropriately specific. Generally, commenting is better than hoping the selector won't notice.

In a sense, this is 'spin', but it's honest spin, or at least it should be (see entry on Selection interviews). This is so for two reasons: pragmatic (you may be closely questioned about it when interviewed) and ethical (consistent with the core counselling quality of genuineness or 'being yourself').

Is it worth saying why you want to do the particular course? Generally, the answer is yes, though our experience is that this is an irrelevant consideration: we've known students who have started the course in sceptical mode, e.g. student S whose motives were unclear but possibly linked to career advancement in teaching and who took a detached, rather cynical approach initially but then became engaged by counselling – excellent selection decision by us! Conversely, there are a few students who begin full of passion and enthusiasm (convincingly conveyed in their application forms and their interviews) but then lose interest. However, most selectors will probably ask you about your motives for choosing counselling and their course, and they will expect sound answers.

assertiveness skills

> ▷ feedback, language, non-verbal communication, self-awareness,
> self-esteem, writing (expressive)

Assertiveness can be defined as 'being able to express and act on your rights as a person while respecting the same rights in others' (Nicolson et al. 2006: 78). It is often seen as a cognitive-behavioural technique (CBT) but is consistent with ideas about being true to oneself from humanistic approaches to counselling. At its heart is the question, 'How much do I do what I want to do and how much do I do what others want me to do?'

Assertiveness theory and skills are relevant to counsellor trainees in two main ways: as a strategy for self-care, and as an option and perspective to consider for some problems with tutors and other students. It is also relevant to several aspects of counselling itself, e.g. setting and maintaining boundaries (Bayne et al. 2008).

Two central assertive skills are making requests and saying no. For example, suppose you want to ask if writing an essay in a particular way is acceptable to a tutor, but are embarrassed (it seems pedantic) or scared (you might look silly) to do so. Such fears might usefully be explored in counselling or in writing, but at the level of actions you could try the assertive skill of making a request.

Thus, you might first check the rights in Table 1. Numbers 2, 3, 8 and 9 – and possibly 10 – are the most likely to be relevant here. Are any of them difficult for you to either believe in or act on? Then you could analyse the potential costs and benefits. If the benefits matter more to you, you next prepare a form of words – a *key phrase* you're comfortable with can be very helpful.

A further preliminary step is to rehearse, in imagination, or using a mirror, or recording yourself, alone or with feedback. At this or another stage you may change your mind (rights 7 and 11). If you wish to continue, the next step is to actually make the request to your tutor. Finally, you may review what happens in a constructive way, looking out for irrational beliefs like 'It's awful when I'm rejected' (cf. right 4) and 'It's terrible to have made such a mess of such a simple thing' (cf. right 6).

Table 1   *Assertive rights*

1. I have the right to be treated with respect	and	Others have the right to be treated with respect
2. I have the right to express my thoughts, opinions and values	and	Others have the right to express their thoughts, opinions and values
3. I have the right to express my feelings	and	Others have the right to express their feelings
4. I have the right to say 'No' without feeling guilty	and	Others have the right to say 'No' without feeling guilty
5. I have the right to be successful	and	Others have the right to be successful
6. I have the right to make mistakes	and	Others have the right to make mistakes
7. I have the right to change my mind	and	Others have the right to change their minds
8. I have the right to say that I don't understand	and	Others have the right to say that they don't understand
9. I have the right to ask for what I want	and	Others have the right to ask for what they want
10. I have the right to decide for myself whether or not I am responsible for another person's problem	and	Others have the right to decide for themselves whether or not they are responsible for another person's problem
11. I have the right to choose not to assert myself	and	Others have the right to choose not to assert themselves

More formally expressed, the basic skill of making a request is as follows:

1 Choose person, request and timing carefully. Consider the possible costs and benefits, your values, your rights and the other person's rights. (A representative sample of assertive rights is in Table 1.)

2 Write out your request, being brief and specific, and checking that it doesn't sabotage itself, i.e. try to convey *and* believe that you don't know the answer (but are hopeful!).

3 Consider including an emotion, e.g. 'I'm embarrassed ...'

4 Rehearse, ideally with coaching from a skilful observer. Check *how* you are making the request: slight adjustments to posture, expression and voice quality can make you look, and probably feel, more assertive.

5 Select time and place (if applicable) to actually make the request.

6 Review what happened. The entries on Rejection, Feedback (receiving and recording) and Decisions may be helpful.

For excellent discussion and vivid examples, see Dickson (1987), which is for both sexes despite its title.

The basic skill of saying no is just as straightforward (in theory):

1 Be brief.
2 Speak clearly and confidently.
3 Rehearse.
4 Select time and place (if applicable)
5 Review.

Dickson (1987) also suggests some useful refinements, e.g.:

- noticing your *first* reaction (to take it into account, though not because it will necessarily be decisive);
- asking for time to think;
- asking for details;
- expressing an emotion;
- offering an alternative;
- calm repetition (if the other person persists).

This approach to assertiveness skills is more consciousness-raising than prescriptive. It emphasises self-awareness, individual style and choices, and being genuine. Assertive rights are one of several complicating factors. Accepting one of the rights can be very enlightening, while ignoring it can be a crucial obstacle. For example, someone might be very angry and upset by a colleague's change of mind but then work through the rights listed in Table 1 and find that number 7 offers a useful perspective. Solutions are not always so easy, of course, but can be achieved.

One way of applying Table 1 is to consider the right-hand column first. Which do you find most difficult to assert? Then consider the left-hand column. Are there any you want to delete (cf. the second right)? Or to add? This list is a composite from Bond (1986), Dickson (1987) and others. The format is from Bond and makes explicit the dual nature of assertiveness: respect for self and respect for others. The last right listed emphasises the point that no one is assertive all the time – though most of us, it seems, would like to be more assertive than we currently are.

The last detailed review of research on assertiveness was many years ago (Rakos 1991). Rakos reviewed hundreds of studies and raised many issues but there has been little research since. He focused mainly on clinical use rather than, like Dickson (1987) and other popular books, on training for people in the general population, and he referred to the clinical use as *therapy* and the personal growth use as *training* (p. 187). He noted the 'extravagant claims' made in some self-help books and remarked that there is a lack of research on their effectiveness and on assertiveness training itself. However, in his view, assertiveness 'is entrenched as a mainstream behavioural intervention; and like other empirically validated techniques, it is quite effective when used appropriately' (p. xi).

assessment of counselling qualities and skills

> ▷ assessment of coursework, de-skilled, presentations, self-awareness, skills versus qualities, strengths

Assessment of counselling qualities and skills can be attempted either by focusing on particular 'assessed sessions', which might be live demonstrations, audio or video recordings, or transcripts of sessions, or some form of ongoing assessment of skills and qualities. An assessed session might also be carried out live, where you will be observed by a tutor and possibly a small panel of peers.

Generally you would be asked to provide some verbal evaluation of the session upon completion and would then receive feedback from tutor and peers. Following on from this, you might need to write an evaluation of the session, taking into account the feedback received. The session will often be recorded to help you to reflect on and evaluate your performance and to allow the assessment to be double-marked.

Whilst this might sound somewhat daunting, most courses which assess skills in these ways include regular practice in skills training groups or 'triads' (groups of three roles: counsellor, client and one or more observers), and these can provide useful opportunities to practise the assessment process and to get helpful feedback before the actual assessment. It is also useful to be aware of the criteria that will be used to assess you. Try to make sure that you understand exactly what skills and qualities you should be demonstrating and that you have a clear sense of what these skills and qualities look like when used effectively. Observation of peers, demonstrations by tutors and recordings of experienced therapists are good opportunities to develop a feel for good practice and a range of potential models for your own development.

Assessment of recorded sessions generally requires the student to submit the recording with a transcript and/or commentary/analysis/evaluation, perhaps of a selected extract. The course may require a recording of some work with someone outside the course group or it may be permissible to use a recording from regular skills training sessions on the course. Either way, it is in your best interest to gather a number of recordings to choose from rather than relying on one. It is also usually worth observing the recordings you have available with the assessment criteria in mind. It's unlikely that you will find the perfect recording – tutors will understand this – but you should pick the one which best demonstrates the assessment criteria. (This might not necessarily be the most impressive or satisfying piece of counselling.)

Most courses base such assessments on a combination of the competence demonstrated on the recording with the quality of analysis and evaluation in your accompanying commentary. Where you are able to identify 'areas for development' in the recording, you have an opportunity to show your awareness of how you might have done things better. You should consider the intention behind your interventions, their impact, suggest alternatives where appropriate, give evidence of your demonstration of required qualities, and show evidence of awareness of the developing relationship between you and the client and the unfolding therapeutic process.

Some courses will ask you to make a presentation of your recorded session to a tutor and perhaps a small group of peers, during which you would play extracts from your recording, provide some commentary and analysis/evaluation, and engage in discussion with the panel. This tends to be a stressful experience (though enjoyable for some), but preparation is likely to help. Plan what you are going to say in advance and practise your presentation so that it sounds coherent and you are confident of the timing. Make sure you are familiar with any technology you will be using, and that you know how to start the recording in the right place, stop it where you want to, etc.

Other strategies for assessment of counselling skills and qualities include logging of case notes/case studies; supervision notes; feedback and reports from supervisors; collecting and analysing evaluation data; logging of skills session notes; ongoing assessment of skills sessions by tutors; and self-appraisal reports. Whilst most of these do not give tutors an opportunity to assess your skills directly, they do give you a variety of opportunities to convince them that you know what you are doing: by collecting and presenting evidence or reflecting on your work in ways which demonstrate self-awareness; by demonstrating an ability to describe, give a rationale for, and evaluate your practice; and by showing evidence of learning and development.

assessment of coursework: issues

> ▷ failing, feedback, plagiarism, references in academic writing, referral, strengths

The first issue to confront is your experience so far of being assessed. You may find it worthwhile making notes about your experiences, including your earliest and most recent, e.g. teachers' remarks, your feelings of rejection, failure, triumph etc., parents' or guardians' reactions to school reports, exam results and so on.

Collect these memories over a few days and then ask yourself about any effects on you now, particularly as you think about the assessment items on your course, and the next one due in. The idea, obviously, is that if you remember feeling hurt and humiliated by earlier experiences of being assessed (and many people, including those who have been academically very successful, do), to try to see them in a new way so that you reduce or end any negative influence on doing future pieces of coursework. You could, for example, talk to a friend, colleague or counsellor, and/or write about them as described in the entry on the Journal.

A second assessment issue (particularly in counsellor training?) is how to balance encouraging the development of individual style with meeting general standards of competence. One strategy is conformity to the norm first, then, as the basic skills and qualities become more familiar and embedded, increasing individuality. However, in our view, critical thinking, developing your own intellectual life, is important from the start.

Third, there is the problem of how clear it is possible and desirable to be about assessment criteria. Can absolute, objective measurable standards of quality be developed? For example, consider the following attempt by one of us to spell out the meaning of different marks for the journal:

DISTINCTION (70%)
- Sophisticated application of the core model
- High level of exploration
- High level of analysis
- Specific actions generated and evaluated very well
- Excellent review: balanced, insightful, high level of critical thinking

VERY GOOD (60–69%)
- Sound application of the core model
- Good level of exploration
- Good level of analysis
- Specific actions generated and evaluated well
- Very good review

PASS (50–59%)
- Coherent but limited application of the core model
- Adequate level of exploration
- Adequate level of analysis
- Specific actions generated and evaluated to a limited extent
- Competent review

REFER (49% OR BELOW)
- Poor application of the core model
- Limited exploration
- Little or no analysis
- Few or no specific actions generated or evaluated
- Review too descriptive and lacking insight

In this attempt, words like 'sophisticated' and 'coherent' are simply alternative expressions for the level of mark they appear to be defining. The assessor still has to make a (professional and informed) judgement. However, the criteria are not a totally spurious exercise: students say they find the listing of qualities useful, that it reduces the mystery a little, or at least appears to. Another positive aspect of general criteria is that they allow or encourage individuality; they can't be treated as mechanically prescriptive and confining.

A related issue is whether counsellor training should be marked Pass/Fail, or Distinction/Pass/Fail, or with a percentage. The assessment policy of an organisation may make any debate irrelevant in practice. Similarly, some colleges and universities require staff to mark anonymously. The aim, of course, is fairness, and perceived fairness. However, it also means that the tutor can't (unless she guesses accurately whose piece of work it is that she's marking) modify her feedback to the student's personality and circumstances. It seems to us inconsistent to ask for personal work and to comment on it when you're not sure who the writer is. Anonymity has much more point with large classes and less personal work.

There are numerous other assessment issues: what is assessed and when; what is not assessed; who assesses (peers?, self?, staff?); the tension between formative assessments, which provide feedback to help students improve, and summative assessments, which count towards the final mark (summative assessment encourages playing safe, not trying out new things and risking not learning from mistakes); the question of what 'messages' assessment items and schemes give students about what they should be learning (these may be obscure or hidden, or interpreted differently by students and staff); and the tension between assessing competence, especially when defined tightly, and encouraging an individual style.

assessment of essays and reports

▷ **assessment of coursework, critical thinking, study skills**

On almost all training courses you will be required to submit some written work in the form of essays or reports. When preparing and writing these it is important to know what the tutors are expecting of you, and in particular what criteria they will be using to assess them. These assessment criteria are likely to be linked to the learning outcomes for the module or unit if your course is organised in that way, which should be available in your course documentation. Generally, any given assessment will be testing a number of the learning outcomes, and the way in which it does this should be evident from the assessment criteria.

While this may seem rather technical from the perspective of a student on a training course, it is to your advantage to know as accurately as possible what it is that you should be demonstrating with each assessment. This will help you to plan your essays or reports and focus your writing. When tutors are briefing you on particular assessments, you may find it helpful to ask some clarification questions to make sure that you understand the assessment criteria.

A number of authors in the educational field have suggested ways of organising learning outcomes and developing assessment criteria (e.g. Anderson and Krathwohl 2001), but as a student the most important thing is that you can understand how to satisfy the criteria in order to pass the assessment or achieve the mark you want.

The main criterion in marking essays and reports is relevance to the title. Consider for example the essay title 'Why are there so many different approaches to counselling?' There is nothing particularly obscure about the wording and yet most essays on it are statements of all the writer knows about person-centred counselling, CBT etc. They don't answer the question. Faced with this essay question, a good strategy is to think of three or four possible reasons for there being many approaches, state them, and use your knowledge of the approaches to illustrate these reasons. This means arguing a case and selecting evidence.

The essays in counselling courses are less likely to be of the traditional kind in which the meaning of the question itself needs to be analysed in some detail. Rather, depth of understanding and levels of critical thinking are tested by how well ideas are *applied*, usually to oneself or to clients. The assessment criteria, naturally, should reflect this, and academic rigour and personal insight given equal weighting.

Assessment criteria are likely to address the following areas.

Knowledge and understanding

You may be required to demonstrate what you *know* in assessments. This could be knowledge of particular facts, principles or theories, but it may also include knowing how to use them or apply them. You can demonstrate this effectively by writing about what you know in context – relating what you have learned to situations in which it applies – and by giving relevant examples of when and how particular knowledge can be used. You may also be required to be able to put your knowledge in a broader context – how particular facts or ideas relate to the historical development of the field or how specific ideas fit into a bigger picture.

Understanding can also be demonstrated by translating ideas in order to apply them to different situations, extrapolating, or comparing and contrasting.

Thinking skills

Some assessment criteria will require that you go beyond knowing things and understanding them, and that you demonstrate your ability to think. This could include things like applying knowledge to new situations and making choices about what to apply when. You can demonstrate this by writing about how you might *assess* and *plan* the way you would approach a particular problem, showing an ability to select appropriately between theories, techniques, approaches etc. Assessment criteria related to thinking skills may also be designed to test your ability to analyse (identify the elements of a given problem or issue, the relationships between them and the principles that apply), synthesise (pull together knowledge from different areas to address a given issue in a comprehensive or new way, or generate alternatives), and evaluate (present judgements about the strength or validity of ideas or approaches, their applicability and limitations, based on evidence or application of some criteria).

Critical thinking is often a key aspect of assessment criteria especially at higher academic levels, and it can be seen as the ability to combine analysis, synthesis and evaluation with a questioning ('What if … ?') approach in the exploration of a particular idea, theory, concept etc. You demonstrate critical thinking by showing awareness of the elements that make something up, exploring how it applies to a range of situations, possibly testing its application in new ways or new situations, looking at how it might be combined with or where it might contradict other ideas, and testing its limits.

Reflection

Assessment criteria for essays and reports (and for journals and professional logs) may also ask you to demonstrate evidence of reflection. You need to show that you have considered the relationship between what is being considered (which may be theories/concepts etc. and/or experiences) and yourself – your thoughts, feelings, behaviours. Reflection involves exploring the impact of an idea or an experience on an individual level, thinking about what it means for you, and its implications. A useful structure for demonstrating reflection is: What? – So what? – Now what?

What?	Describe the experience (which might include encountering a new idea, concept, theory etc.). How did you respond (thoughts, feelings, behaviour)?
So what?	What might this mean to you? What can you learn from it? What new insights are available to you (e.g. patterns in your thinking/feeling/behaviour; alternatives; strengths, areas for development etc.)?
Now what?	What might you like to do or do differently as a result of reflection? Identify goals or action plans that might follow and consider how you will evaluate progress.

The notion of the *reflective practitioner* is important in counselling and psychotherapy, and you will need to be able to demonstrate in some of your assessments that you are self-aware and self-challenging. In other words, you must show that you can identify and monitor your thoughts, feelings and behaviour; that you are aware of your patterns and preferences, strengths and limitations; that you can evaluate your work in terms of what has gone well and what could have gone better, and identify possible alternatives in the latter case; and that as a result of reflection you can identify appropriate learning and development goals for yourself, and generate action plans to achieve these goals.

Evidence of practical skills

Some essays or reports may also have assessment criteria that require you to provide evidence of your practical skills, for example in client work, or making use of supervision. To do this you may find it useful to think in terms of *description* and *evaluation*. The former means that you provide a clear enough account of what you did to convince the assessor that you know what you are talking about. So for example, rather than saying 'I used CBT', you would need to provide some detail of *how* you explored the thoughts a client experienced in a given situation, how these impacted on their feelings and behaviour, and how you went about helping the client to change them. You are then in a position to evaluate your use of skills. What was the impact? How effective was it? What worked well and what could have gone better? What alternatives can you suggest? Thoughtful evaluation provides further evidence that you understand what you are doing and can discern the level of competence you are demonstrating.

assessment of presentations

▷ **assessment of coursework, feedback (giving), presentations**

The scales below are one way of assessing presentations and giving feedback on them. They can also, of course, be helpful when preparing and making a presentation.

	Very						*Not very*
Voice quality							
Audible?	7	6	5	4	3	2	1
Clear?							
Varied in tone?							
Other comments?							
Content							
Well-structured?							
Clear?							
Useful?							
Good example?							
Helpful visual aids?							
Other comments?							
Questions							
Listened to well?							
Answered well?							
Other comments?							

attendance requirement

▷ **trust**

Counselling courses accredited by BACP (British Association for Counselling and Psychotherapy) are required to monitor students' attendance and to implement an 80 per cent limit. One view is that this puts the emphasis in the wrong place: on hours present rather than on quality of outcome. However, for the group to function well, it needs diverse contributions and for people to trust each other, and both are more achievable if students are present.

b

beginning of a course

▷ boredom, exercises, expectations, fears, imagery, open circle, trust

The beginning of a counselling course is full of mystery, hopes and fears. From the first session (and before), the tutors aim to create a good 'atmosphere' for counsellor training, which means in part students trusting each other and the tutors, and feeling both calm and alert most of the time. It's probably helpful if the tutors are themselves fairly calm and alert (warm, genuine and businesslike also seem useful qualities here).

The terms 'support' and 'challenge' describe part of what is involved, and you may find them a helpful way of thinking about what's going on and perhaps about what you'd like to be different. They imply a model of four possibilities:

1 High support and high challenge (stimulating and safe).

2 High support and low challenge (too comfortable – may not be much work done).

3 Low support and high challenge (too taxing – people may become defensive).

4 Low support and low challenge (too boring – may become apathetic or leave).

If you suspect that a course is wrong for you in terms of this model, or for some other reason, some possible next steps are described in the entries on Decisions, Writing (expressive) and Journal.

As another perspective on beginning a course, we next list several introductory exercises, chosen for variety from hundreds of possibilities. Your reactions of interest, boredom, fear etc. to these may help you prepare for the real thing, choose a course, or choose not to train as a counsellor either at all or for the time being.

Examples of the many techniques that can be used to contribute to the course atmosphere, to set the tone from the start, are shown on the following page. However, other factors, e.g. pace and tone, or a particular exchange, may matter more than the exercise itself.

> ‣ Talk about your name, its cultural significance and its significance to you.
> ‣ Write down (a) your previous experience of counsellor training, e.g. one-day courses; (b) your self-directed learning about counselling, e.g. books, TV programmes, voluntary work etc. Then exchange information with one or two partners and help each other describe your present level of experience, e.g. 'I'm a beginner' or 'At the moment I feel comfortable with this kind of client, these skills, these ideas.' Finally, help each other describe what you hope to learn from the course.
> ‣ 'New and good': each person, usually in a circle, says something that's new and good in their lives. The rest of the group listen and don't comment.
> ‣ Discuss the 'ground rules' you'd like to be followed in this group.
> ‣ Have rules presented to you.
> ‣ Do a visualisation exercise (see entry on Imagery).
> ‣ Choose a more 'organic' approach in which the tutor doesn't take the lead.
> ‣ In pairs, talk about your thoughts and feelings about the beginning but treat what is said as confidential and *don't* discuss them.
> ‣ In groups of four or five, discover what you have in common (and report back to the main group).
> ‣ Write notes about your experience now and then talk about those aspects you feel comfortable to talk about in groups of three or four.

One way in which tutors can model warmth and reduce some mystery is to join in the exercises themselves. However, self-disclosure of this kind is much more consistent with some counselling orientations than with others, and more desirable and practical with some exercises than others.

Perhaps the main thing to say about the beginning of a course is that it will be new and possibly strange and that you can feel overwhelmed; but that usually people find a rhythm and feel increasingly supported and challenged. In this respect, beginning a course is very much like the first steps in developing a counselling relationship.

beginning of each training day

▷ open circle

'best books'

▷ clinical wisdom, reading lists

'body language'

▷ non-verbal communication

boredom in teaching sessions

▷ assertiveness, expectations, self-awareness, stress, study skills, trust, writing (expressive)

b

You may be bored in one or more sessions of your course and, if you are, we think it's worth taking seriously. Surprisingly, given that it's probably quite a frequent experience and presumably a block to learning, boredom in adult students hasn't been studied much. The only studies we know of are Marsh (1983) and Mann and Robinson (2009).

Marsh used Interpersonal Process Recall (IPR – see separate entry) with four students and two tutors. She videoed one of a series of workshops on a course for management trainees, then acted as Inquirer with each participant in turn. The recall sessions each lasted over two hours, and the inquirees found the technique, which was new to them, fun and exciting. In contrast, the main finding from the recalls was that 'the overwhelming sense that pervaded everything was one of boredom. Everyone described feelings of boredom, lack of energy about the task, or the group' (p. 125).

Marsh comments that she wasn't surprised and no one else seemed to be either. She had often felt bored herself as a student and as a tutor. It was also clear that the students believed the others were bored too, but that none of them attempted to examine why or to do anything about it. 'They just wished things were different' (p. 125).

The kind of boredom experienced most often was called 'emotional-motivational', by which Marsh meant 'coming from fears and insecurities ... and also fear of revealing their feelings to the group or to the tutor (p. 128). Marsh also found that expectations about the roles of student and tutor were influential, e.g. 'it was the look-interested bit coming through, even if you aren't, just play along'. Concerns not to hurt the tutors' feelings and to behave 'acceptably' were mentioned. Moreover, the boredom itself seemed to be expressed as disabling: it was described as 'lethargy', 'being trapped', 'a mental bog' etc.

Marsh comments that boredom is not necessarily bad; it can be a step in clarifying a mismatch between expectations about a course/teaching style and what actually happens, and then seeing the benefits of the different style. In the teaching session she investigated, the clash was between expecting a passive student role, tutor in control, with an experiential actual style. A second issue is how easy it is for students to 'play a game of please-the-tutor, to feign attention, apparent energy and interest, while in fact being bored, uninterested and inattentive' (p. 134).

Mann and Robinson (2009) surveyed 211 university students of a wide range of subjects. Fifty-nine per cent of the students said (anonymously) that they found at least half of their lectures boring and almost a third said they found all or nearly all their lectures boring. This is much too high, although a limitation of their methodology noted by the authors was that these were retrospective estimates; different, perhaps lower, proportions might result from asking students immediately after lectures.

For students, the implications are to assess the causes of your feeling bored and to consider how best to cope with them. The most popular ways of coping found in Mann and Robinson's survey were daydreaming, doodling, chatting and texting – are they the most effective? In addition, you may like to consider how much your personality contributes – Mann and Robinson found that 'boredom proneness' was the most important factor predicting boredom in lectures. If you are highly prone to boredom, what might you do to manage it?

One factor is preferred methods of learning, and generally practical sessions and group discussions seem to be more engaging, or at least less boring (Mann and Robinson 2009). These teaching methods are probably more widely used in counselling courses than in most subjects although lectures have tended to become more interactive in the last few years too, with exercises, buzz groups, thought experiments etc. It may therefore be worth asking in detail about the teaching methods used by a course you're considering.

We see two further implications of these two studies for tutors and students on counselling courses particularly. First, clear communication is at the heart of counselling, communication about *anything*: the aim is no taboo topics to fester and block (Bayne et al. 2008); and counsellor training needs to aim for this ideal too. So we want to encourage openness about and responsibility for feelings. Second, it is probably inevitable that the teaching methods that some students find appealing, others will find boring, wholly or in part. This may be eased through using the three-stage model of counselling discussed in the entry on the Journal. What we don't want in our sessions is undue pretence and stoicism.

boundaries

▷ assertiveness, ethics, trust

Being able to maintain appropriate boundaries is an important element of your development as a counsellor. The term is usually used to refer to the boundaries of the counsellor–client relationship (see below) but the establishment and maintenance of boundaries is important in a number of areas. A boundary is a line that separates areas which are in some way different, and in the context of counselling training the difference often lies in the ground rules or conventions that apply on either side. Some examples of important boundaries are:

- *Between inside the course and outside.* It will generally be expected that there will be a confidentiality boundary around the course, so that what goes on within the group is not material for discussion at home, at work, etc. Courses vary in how they specify this boundary – in some cases, for instance, it may be agreed that it is permissible to discuss the activities which take place on the course, but not the content of discussions or problems brought by group members. It is important that group members feel able to share in an environment of trust, and can be sure that what they have chosen to share is not communicated to others outside the group.

▸ *Between sub-groups on the course and the whole group.* You should not automatically assume that because someone has chosen to discuss a problem in a sub-group (e.g. skills training or supervision), they are happy for it to be aired in the whole group. For this reason there are normally ground rules establishing the boundaries between different groupings on a course.

▸ *Between your role as a trainee counsellor and other roles in your life.* Many students become enthusiastic about their developing skills (which is probably a good thing) and want to practise them at every opportunity (which may be less of a good thing). It is important to establish some boundaries for yourself to avoid the temptation to 'counsel' family members, friends, colleagues etc. every time they seem to present an opportunity. This can be tiresome for those who do not want to be 'counselled', and it can create precedents which you may later regret if people are frequently expecting you to help them with their problems after initial enthusiasm has waned.

Whilst it is probably inevitable (and indeed only human) that you will use some of your skills to assist those you care about on occasions, you cannot ethically be a counsellor to friends, relatives and colleagues. This is, at least in part, because your established relationship and knowledge of each other will frequently be a barrier to the development of a therapeutic relationship. If you are part of someone's life in other ways, then you will have your own perspectives on the problems that are troubling them – you may even have a role in those problems.

▸ *Between your time with clients and other parts of your life.* If you are able to develop genuine empathic relationships with clients then you will share in their emotional experience, and you will need to learn to manage the impact this has on you. Given that clients are often experiencing emotions such as anger, pain and sadness, there is a danger of becoming weighed down with negative emotion, and carrying it into other areas of your life. The nature of the counselling relationship precludes attempts at 'professional detachment' and emotional distancing. Counsellors have to learn to be open to experiencing feelings empathically and genuinely with clients within the boundaries of a session, but then to move on from them after a session in order to either engage with the next client, or engage with other aspects of life such as family, friends and leisure.

Most counsellors find the practice of the 50-minute 'therapy hour' helpful in this respect. The remaining 10 minutes can be used for writing brief notes (which may in itself help to 'contain' the session) or engaging in activities or 'rituals' that enable disengagement from the session that has just finished. Strategies used can include the informal (e.g. cup of tea, some fresh air), cognitive (e.g. identifying three ways I am different from the client), brief meditations, relaxation exercises or visualisations. This is an area you might usefully discuss in supervision to monitor and evaluate how you are maintaining this boundary.

In spite of our best efforts to manage the impact of our clients' emotions and stories, most of us will find that some clients at some times will break through our defences. We then find ourselves feeling sad or preoccupied, upset or concerned after a session, and perhaps for some time afterwards. This is probably inevitable and 'goes with the territory', but you should (a) be aware that it will happen occasionally and develop some strategies for coping when it does, (b) monitor how often it happens and evaluate your coping strategies, and (c) discuss it in supervision when it does happen – it is important to determine whether there are particular 'buttons' being pushed which you need to work on in supervision, personal therapy or expressive writing.

▸ *Around the counsellor–client relationship*. The therapeutic relationship is unusual in many ways and, as a result, care is needed in maintaining appropriate boundaries. Whilst many approaches to counselling strive to make the relationship 'equal' in the sense of being collaborative, the client and counsellor have distinct roles.

The relationship exists to help the client. So while the client is likely to disclose personal information, some of which might be quite sensitive or intimate, inappropriate self-disclosure on the part of the counsellor can be unhelpful for the client if it shifts their attention away from their own issues. The counsellor is in a professional role and the boundaries established should reflect this, in that the relationship is different to friendship or a social relationship. As a counsellor, you have a responsibility to provide a safe frame within which the client can feel understood and accepted, and experience trust in you without risk of exploitation. You need to make sure that your own needs for friendship and intimacy are being met in other areas of your life and not allow them to blur the boundaries of your therapeutic relationships.

The therapeutic relationship also has time boundaries – you meet your clients for a contracted time and are not part of their lives outside of that. Care needs to be taken about start and end times for sessions, particularly if clients seem to find it difficult to hold time boundaries for themselves.

Different approaches may have different 'rules' or guidelines about how strictly time boundaries need to be held but, from a practical point of view, if you are working to an appointment schedule there is unlikely to be much space for overrunning the scheduled end of a session.

Holding time boundaries is also part of providing a safe frame for a client. Uncertainty about ending times can lead to confusion and anxiety, and whilst some clients may seem to challenge ending times by introducing new and perhaps emotive or difficult material late in a session, they may be doing so precisely because there is a limit on the time available to work with it. We would not go so far as to say that it is never appropriate to extend a session, but we would see it as a response to exceptional circumstances, and suggest that you should be clear about the reasons for doing so, the amount of extra time to be taken, and the therapeutic goals involved (Bayne et al. 2008).

There may also be issues around contact or communication outside the contracted sessions. Ground rules may be needed about means of communication which do not compromise you or the client if sessions need to be cancelled or rearranged, or in case of emergencies, and you may also need to discuss with clients how to respond if you should encounter each other 'outside'. If you are seeing your clients through an agency, it is likely they will have policies and procedures in place to address these issues and you should, of course, make sure you are familiar with them.

Confidentiality is an important issue for many clients in order to develop trust. Again, the boundaries need to be clear, both to reassure the client that what they talk about will not be shared inappropriately and to make sure they understand that confidentiality between counsellor and client is not absolute. You will need to talk about your work in supervision, and if a danger to the client or another becomes apparent in a session you may need to consider breaching confidentiality if the client is not willing to take appropriate steps (see BACP 2009b; Bond 2009).

Dependence is an issue that concerns some trainee counsellors and is related to maintaining appropriate boundaries. The responsibility of feeling that a client is dependent on you may weigh heavily, perhaps as holiday times approach, or you may begin to worry that the client will always be dependent on you. Such concerns need to be discussed in supervision. While it is clearly the aim of counselling to help clients to become more autonomous and empowered, we think it is inevitable that clients may at times value the counselling relationship to such an extent that they might be said to be dependent on it. This is not necessarily unhealthy if it is a temporary situation, as long as the general direction of the work with the client is in the direction of developing their own strengths and resources.

brochures, course

> ▷ fees and funding, hours of study, qualifications

Hunt (1996) analysed 69 course brochures and prospectuses and her impression was that they 'were often difficult to read and sometimes so discursively written it was difficult to extract the "hard" information' (p. 202). By 'hard' she meant the details potential students tend to need in order to make a decision about whether to apply or not: time commitments, staff numbers and qualifications, fees and other costs, and so on (see the checklist in this entry). Kwiatkowski (1998) also felt 'rather frustrated' when extracting this kind of information from the publicity material and, further, found 'little relation between what courses were called and their entry requirements, need for prior experience, or personal therapy, or cost, or the time required for completion' (p. 13).

Quality of publicity material may have improved or at least become more glossy in the last few years because of a much greater emphasis on marketing and competition. The following checklist is intended to help you decide which information is helpful to you, either from a course brochure or, if it's vague or lacking, from the staff:

- The organisation
- The core model or models
- The level and aims of the course
- Its length and structure
- Its content
- Time commitments
- Assessment items
- Selection procedure
- Policy on equal opportunities
- Fees and other costs
- Numbers of students
- Staff members, experience and qualifications
- Teaching methods

C

careers in counselling

> ▷ choosing a career, counselling and coaching, counselling and psychotherapy, future, strengths

Forging a career in counselling is something of a challenge and you would be wise to explore the options available before embarking on a training course. Unlike many other helping professions, there is not as yet a clear career structure or ladder for counsellors. A number of historical factors have contributed to this, including the tendency in the UK for a relatively high proportion of counselling to have been provided through the voluntary sector, the willingness of qualified counsellors to continue to work without pay whilst accumulating client hours towards professional accreditation, and the tendency for counselling to be a second career so that counsellors could earn income in other ways whilst developing their counselling practice.

This has meant that for many counsellors the most difficult step in their career has been the transition from voluntary to paid work. The tendency has been for counsellors to make this transition in a rather gradual way, if at all. This might involve continuing to earn money through employment in a previous role, gradually moving from full-time to part-time work whilst building up some counselling work on a sessional basis with a service or agency, or with a small number of private clients. This might lead on to part-time employment as a counsellor or developing a private practice whilst continuing to reduce the time spent on previous employment. Many have chosen to reach an equilibrium point where they spend part of their time working as a counsellor and part doing other things, on the basis that they are achieving a better balance in their lives this way than working full time as a counsellor. (Note that it is recommended that even full-time counsellors should only spend 18–20 hours per week actually seeing clients.)

However, there has been and continues to be a gradual trend towards more career opportunities for counsellors as counselling becomes embedded in the National Health Service, schools and the workplace, and the evidence base for its effectiveness strengthens. Agencies are developing and growing in both the public and provide sectors that employ counsellors and provide services in health and social care, education, and occupational health/EAPs (Employee Assistance Programmes). You may find it useful to check the employment opportunities section of the BACP website on a regular basis, even if you are not actively seeking paid work, in order to familiarise yourself with the kinds of jobs that are being advertised, rates of pay, and expectations of potential employers regarding experience and qualifications.

Careful (or fortunate) choice of a practice placement during your training can help get you started with building a career. Some placement providers may offer paid work to students who have completed their training, while working for an agency or service which has a good reputation can enhance your CV when applying for jobs elsewhere.

Alternatively, you may wish to pursue your career aspirations via private practice. This involves all of the complications of setting up a small business, and is likely to build slowly since it takes time to establish a reputation. It can, of course, be a rewarding and successful venture – or very frustrating (Feltham 1995, 2002; Bayne et al. 2008). Again, you should probably plan for a gradual transition whereby you build up your practice as best you can whilst earning your main income from some other employment, which is then gradually reduced.

case studies, writing

▷ **critical thinking, ethics, language, process reports, self-awareness**

It is likely that as part of the assessment for your training programme you will be required to submit one or more written pieces of work which are a reflection and analysis of your work with a client. These may or may not be called 'case studies' and some would argue that this is not the ideal term since it seems to imply that it is a study of the client. However, regardless of the name, you should be aware that what is required is more likely to focus on *your work with the client* rather than the details of the client's history, issues and so on. As with all written assessments, you should read the assessment criteria carefully and make sure that you approach the work in a way that addresses these directly. In our experience, case study assessments are mainly focused on asking you to demonstrate:

- your appropriate application of qualities, skills, techniques and approaches;
- your ability to account for what you have done (i.e. give a rationale for the way you have worked which includes collaboration with the client in assessment, identification of therapeutic goals, and ongoing therapeutic planning);
- your self-awareness as you work with the client, monitoring and using your own emotions and responses, and addressing any issues which arise in an appropriate forum such as supervision or personal therapy;
- your ability to work within an appropriate ethical framework, and maintain therapeutic boundaries;
- your ability to manage issues of difference and equality;

- ‣ your ability to reflect on your work, including the development and dynamics of the therapeutic relationship, identifying learning, strengths, and areas for development;
- ‣ your ability to evaluate your work, including eliciting feedback from the client.

In order to do this effectively you will, of course, have to include some information about the client, their story, issues, responses, progress and their part in the therapeutic relationship. You should make sure that you have obtained appropriate permission from the client and the placement where you are seeing them to use this material in a case study, and you should ensure that names and any other personal information that might allow the client to be identified are changed. However, we suggest that you only include enough client information to enable the reader to make sense of your account of your work, to make an informed judgement about the appropriateness of your approach and interventions and the quality of your analysis, reflection, etc.

You will not have the space to write a detailed narrative of all of your work with a client and the value of doing so would in any case be limited. Rather, it will be necessary to make some editorial choices about what to cover relatively briefly and what aspects of your work to focus on in more detail in order to demonstrate what is required by the assessment criteria. An account which attends to key moments in your work in considerable detail and specificity, and summarises other aspects relatively succinctly, is more likely to be effective in demonstrating high standards than one which attempts to maintain a uniform level of detail.

So, in planning a case study you should try to decide which sessions or parts of sessions are most significant to the overall course of therapy, and best illustrate the way you were working, the relationship with your client, and the other required criteria. You can then structure your case study as a more detailed analysis of these key episodes, linked by summaries of what happened in between.

Try to avoid using technical or jargon terms as an alternative to describing what you actually did. So, rather than saying 'I used CBT', give an explanation of how you worked with particular thoughts, feelings and behaviours; and rather than saying 'I maintained a non-judgemental approach', give an example of what you said or did that would communicate this quality to your client. (Similarly, you should focus more on describing how your client communicated and behaved and avoid applying diagnostic labels to them, except perhaps to note when diagnoses have been made by other professionals.)

Brief transcript extracts are useful in case studies to give a flavour of the interaction with the client and bring your account to life. A useful format is to include a statement by the client, followed by your intervention, followed by the client's response. For example:

Client:	I'm so fed up at work now. I have to do so much that just feels meaningless. I sometimes feel like packing it in or going part time and looking for something different.
Counsellor:	You sound really hopeless when you say that, and it's like it's really grinding you down. And yet you do have some ideas about how you might change things.
Client:	Well yes I do, and when I think about it I'm not really sure what's keeping me there.

This gives you the opportunity to explain the rationale for the intervention you chose in the context of the session, the relationship and the overall course of your work with the client; to reflect on the impact it had; and perhaps to consider alternatives.

Many students find it easier to write about the content of therapy (what the client brings and talks about) rather than the process, but a good counselling case study generally requires less of the former and more of the latter. To achieve this, it might be helpful to ask yourself some of the following questions:

- How did the client come to counselling?
- How did we identify the issues we were to work on and the goals for therapy?
- How much did we talk about the way we would work together?
- How did the therapeutic relationship begin, and develop?
- What factors about me and the client influenced the way we related to each other?
- How did the relationship change and evolve? Were there particular moments when it changed, when problems arose or when it moved to a different level (within particular sessions or across the time we worked together)?
- At particular moments, and overall, what impact did I have on the client, and what impact did the client have on me?
- What approaches, techniques and interventions did I use? And why?
- How effective were they?
- What difficulties or dilemmas arose and how did I manage them?
- What did I take to supervision and what did I learn or do differently as a result?
- How did I involve the client in ongoing therapeutic planning and evaluation?
- How did the relationship end?

choosing a career

Surveys of 'job satisfaction' suggest that most people in the UK have a job that suits them (Doyle 2003). However, chance and opportunity are powerful factors in finding or devising a career that fits, and how many people *choose* their work in a meaningful sense is arguable. Moreover, the term 'satisfied' is fairly bland when choice of career can be about fulfilment and feeling engaged.

Two counter-arguments here are that for some people their work is a way of earning money – what they do outside work matters much more – and that others find the idea of fulfilment itself unengaging. They don't, to use an American term popular with some careers experts, resonate to it and they might resonate even less to another popular phrase: 'finding your passion'. However, terms like 'fascinating', 'finding your place in life', and 'deeply interesting' may make more sense and be more appealing , and all these terms imply that a matching between personality and kind of work is desirable (Bayne 2004).

There are several approaches to choosing a career that suits you:

- Experimenting and gradually discovering what you enjoy (and are sufficiently, employably, good at) and what you don't enjoy.
- Speeding up this process by increasing self-awareness in other ways, and especially by focusing on strengths.

And then there are less direct approaches:

- Using a website like www.prospects.ac.uk.
- Remembering jobs you fantasised about as a child (or now).
- Remembering what you most enjoyed doing as a child (and if you have interests or hobbies that you enjoy now).
- Asking what would you happily do for no salary if you could afford to.
- Asking people who know you well for their ideas and observations about your personal qualities and interests.

The next step with these less direct strategies is to reflect on them seriously and, less obviously, to write your thoughts and feelings down: What exactly is it you enjoy or might enjoy about them? Can you investigate them further? And then the practicalities, e.g. what careers might they be relevant to? Can you be more precise? For example, if you want to write, what kind of writing and where is it published? Can you separate the complication that interests may be more a reflection of parents', guardians' or peers' influence than from you? And what can you do about the thought (perhaps too romantic) that there may be an ideal career for you that you've never heard of or have wrongly rejected?

Other complications are that in many jobs there is sufficient variation for people of different personalities, interests and strengths to find a fulfilling niche

(Bayne 2004), and that new jobs are being created and old ones disappearing. If you're clear that a career in counselling – either full time or part of a portfolio of work – is right for you, the next two entries are intended to help you choose a counselling orientation (and therefore, in part, a course).

choosing a counselling orientation

> ▷ choosing a counselling orientation: the role of personality, counselling and coaching, counselling and psychotherapy, decisions, integrative counselling, membership organisations, metaphors, motives, strengths, values

Counselling orientation is a relatively unimportant factor in how effective counselling is. Other factors, like the client's readiness to change and the therapeutic relationship, matter much more (Lambert 2004; Cooper 2008). Nevertheless, it probably still plays a part through affecting the counsellor's ease and confidence, and there is also the possibility that *interactions* between orientation, client personality and problem contribute, though this level of complexity is hard to investigate well.

Thus, initial choice of orientation is important for trainees and people considering training. As Scragg et al. (1999) suggested: making a poor decision 'can be costly in terms of time, money and low morale among trainees and tutors' (p. 263).

For discussion of the various orientations or approaches, see McLeod (2009). Briefly, each of the over 400 approaches so far suggested can be grouped in one (or sometimes more) of four main categories: psychodynamic, humanistic, cognitive-behavioural and transpersonal. Key concepts which illustrate the main emphasis of each of these four categories are the 'dynamic unconscious' (psychodynamic), 'becoming oneself' or self-actualisation (humanistic), 'irrational beliefs' (cognitive-behavioural) and 'higher self' (transpersonal). In addition, there are integrative or eclectic approaches (see entries on Integration and Integrative counselling).

Several factors can be involved in the decision, e.g. a model's popularity, ease of travelling to a course, availability of places. Evi Varlami, as part of a study described in Varlami and Bayne (2007), analysed responses from 84 students (with an average age of 35 years) on counselling psychology courses to the following question: 'Please use the space below [half an A4 page] to describe how you have come to your choice of Theoretical Orientation. What factors do you believe influenced you most in your choices?'

A majority of the participants (45 of 84) cited their personality as the main factor in their choice. For example, one stated: 'In therapy, you just have to be yourself. If the model you are working with does not fit your personality you won't practice well enough. I had to think of my behaviour and personality and chose CBT.' Another wrote 'Person-centred theory best fits my personality, as I think it is very important especially for a counselling psychologist to practice in a way that they behave in real life. Theories of psychology for me are theories of life really.'

The next most influential factor, in the view of the participants, was interpreted as referring indirectly to personality. For example, 'I prefer working with feelings' and 'I have always been working with CBT, I think I prefer having a structure in sessions.' Twenty-one participants (25 per cent) made this kind of comment.

Three other factors, seen as minor (cited by 4–12 participants each), were the supervisor's influence, e.g. 'From the very beginning I had a CBT supervisor and I didn't feel safe to go my way'; training, e.g. 'My initial training was Person-centred and I followed it ever since'; and placement requirements, e.g. 'In my placement, I have to work CBT.'

Thus, choice of orientation seems to be developmental, with personality being the most influential factor, directly and indirectly. The last respondent's use of 'have to' appears to be a pragmatic acceptance of situation versus ideal choice, but perhaps also suggests that the factors involved in choosing an orientation and placement should be emphasised more in counsellor training (Arthur 2001).

A possible bias in the methodology of Varlami's research is that the covering letter to participants stated that we were investigating whether personality characteristics are associated with choice of orientation. Participants may have been influenced by this statement. On the other hand, we did place the personality questionnaire after the open-ended question and the participants' responses to it were detailed and seemed genuine. Further research on choosing counselling orientation could examine the process in more detail, through interviewing, for example, and through exploring the relevance of relationships and personality.

choosing a counselling orientation: the role of personality

▷ choosing a counselling orientation, psychological type

The quite extensive research on counselling orientation and personality should not be applied prescriptively or rigidly. Rather, the research suggests that different orientations (or, probably, elements within orientations) tend to suit people with certain personality characteristics and not to suit others (Dodd and Bayne 2006; Ogunfowora and Drapeau 2008). Thus, it does not follow that people with the 'wrong personality' for a particular model should avoid it. Rather, they would probably benefit from examining their motives with particular care but they might also contribute in unusual ways to the development of the model or find a niche within it.

Dodd and Bayne (2006) found, in a sample of 123 experienced counsellors, clear personality differences between those who chose CBT, psychoanalytic, psychosynthesis and integrative counselling models. Choice of person-centred model was not related to personality in this sample, though it was in Varlami and Bayne's (2007) sample of trainee counselling psychologists.

We don't want to be more specific here about the personality characteristics studied because we want to avoid any possible negative effects on course sessions on personality. It may be better to come to these fresh. It is obvious, though, that we (like Arthur 2001 and others) recommend taking personality into account when choosing an orientation.

There are criticisms of this view: e.g. Lazarus (1978) challenged it as 'stereotyping' – limiting both the potential of counsellors and each model's complexities. We recognise stereotyping as a danger, but emphasise the value of informed choices by trainees. Moreover, Lazarus himself is probably far more eclectic than most counsellors would be comfortable being.

Another source of information about choice of orientation and personality is autobiography, e.g. Spinelli and Marshall (2001), in which expert practitioners from a wide range of orientations discuss how their lives express their chosen theory. Windy Dryden, for example, trained in person-centred and psychoanalytic therapies 'but neither of these therapeutic approaches resonated with me as much as REBT did, and still does' (p. 28). He analyses the way that REBT (rational emotive behaviour therapy) is related to elements of his personality such as activity level, self-discipline, self-reliance, cognitive and philosophic orientations, and humour. In a thoughtful commentary on the other chapters, Spinelli and Marshall suggest two main ways in which their authors 'chose' or 'found' their models: 'those for whom the model confirmed previously held ideas, and those for whom such earlier concepts were altered, expanded on or even demolished by the model in question' (p. 166).

choosing a counsellor

> ▷ choosing a counselling orientation, personal development, personal
> therapy

Choosing a counsellor is a complex decision, and one which we suggest should be approached thoughtfully and step by step. You might become aware of available counsellors through your course, by personal recommendation, through directories (for example BACP) or advertising. Advice is available on the BACP website: http://www.bacp.co.uk/seeking_therapist/right_therapist. php

Most counsellors will offer an initial meeting or assessment session, which will enable both of you to explore what you might work on and how you might work together, and this is as much an opportunity for you to assess your potential therapist as it is for them to assess you. You should be trying to get a sense of what sort of relationship you might develop and what it might be like sharing and working with this person.

You may find it helpful to keep in mind the research on the effectiveness of counselling (Hubble et al. 1999; Lambert 2004) and the key factors identified. Factors relating to the client (such as readiness to engage in counselling, strengths and support available) have the greatest influence on the outcome. This suggests that you should think carefully first about your own readiness to engage in the process and your strengths and support. In an initial meeting with a potential counsellor you might also want to bear in mind the extent to which they seem interested in these factors.

Relationship factors are the next most important in Lambert's (2004) framework, so you might also reflect carefully on the prospect of developing a relationship based on empathy, warmth and acceptance with your potential therapist. The relationship *as perceived by the client* is the key here, so you are entitled and indeed recommended to pay attention to your own responses and feelings. Expectancy and placebo effects are important too, so you might also pay attention to how positive and optimistic about therapy you feel after meeting with a potential counsellor.

Model and technique factors have some influence on positive outcomes in therapy, but less so than the other factors above. This is in contrast with our experience of students (and others) when they are choosing a counsellor, where often the first consideration seems to be, 'I want someone who works in a person-centred (or cognitive or psychodynamic etc.) way ...'. There may be some value as a trainee therapist in gaining experience as a client working with a particular approach, but be aware that in terms of positive outcomes from therapy, model/technique factors only account for about 15 per cent of improvement (Lambert 2004). Hubble et al. (1999) suggest that models and techniques which are a good fit with the client's existing framework for understanding themselves and the processes of change and development are most likely to be successful, so you may wish to explore your own 'personal models' as a guide to the orientation of potential therapists.

A final factor to consider is the issue of you, a trainee counsellor, engaging as a client with your therapist and how that might influence the relationship and process. Some students have experienced or perceived difficulties arising from this, such as the counsellor's expectations, attitude or level of comfort/confidence. This may well be another useful area to explore in an initial meeting.

choosing a course to apply for

▷ beginning of a course, boredom, choosing a counselling orientation, core model, decisions, membership organisations, study skills

client, preparing for the training role of

▷ assertiveness, distressed, self-awareness

Most counsellor training courses ask trainees to practise counselling with each other, and therefore, for part of the time, to be a client. Most courses, we suspect, also ask the clients to talk about real problems because it is confusing for the counsellor to work with made-up or exaggerated problems, at least not without challenging them. Counselling is at its heart about clarifying real emotions and thoughts.

Therefore trainee counsellors need topics that they are willing to talk about, sometimes with very little warning. We suggest three possibilities. The first is being open to 'what is on top' (a co-counselling phrase). Thus, if you feel upset, confused or angry (say) about an incident, e.g. a news item, that might be a suitable topic for you to talk about as a practice client. Second, you might keep a list of topics. Your list might include some trustworthy 'favourites', e.g. a particular relationship, but can also be updated as issues are resolved or become less important, and of course as new ones arise.

Third, you might like to complete sentence stems like these:

> ‣ I dislike people who …
> ‣ I like people who …
> ‣ I want …
> ‣ I envy …
> ‣ In relationships, I …
> ‣ I daydream about …
> ‣ I get angry about …
> ‣ I regret …

Two general principles seem important here. For most practice sessions, a 'medium level' problem is probably best: neither superficial nor too demanding for your counsellor at their stage of development. However, if the counselling is effective, you may go deeper quite quickly, and we would like participants to accept that. There's one proviso, which is the second general principle: if you feel too upset or 'wrong', we would like you to say so (an assertiveness skill) and not to press on.

A further option here is to use 'attention out', a co-counselling technique which is in effect the opposite of counselling. You direct your attention outwards or at least away from your emotions, e.g. looking for all the green things in the room or counting the number of objects or counting backwards in sevens from 303 (say). It's a simple distraction or redirection of attention technique but effective. Attention out can be used as self-help or offered to someone else.

'clinical wisdom'

▷ **critical thinking, evidence-based practice**

We've found for ourselves how valuable the views about counselling and life of experienced practitioners and others can be. In a 'sticky moment', or reflecting on a problematic counselling session, they can be dramatically useful: they can give a new perspective or suggest some options. They could even be the difference between surviving counsellor training and leaving it.

One of the purposes of reading the counselling literature is to find those gems of clinical wisdom that work for you. The gems are mainly part of the artistic element in counselling, and therefore need, we think, to be approached with critical thinking principles in mind: both trusting and sceptical. Being firmly convinced that something is true doesn't make it true!

Sometimes a gem is an empirical finding, but usually it's a principle of practice. We find Yalom (1989, 2001) an excellent source, although we also think that some of his suggestions are not true or rarely true.

Here are three examples of what to us are gems of clinical wisdom:

'I always listen carefully to first statements.' (Yalom 1989: 16)

'It is not your responsibility to solve your client's problem.' (Source unknown)

'Reviewing the first ten years of my psychotherapy practice, I found that most of my therapeutic failures resulted from working too hard and saying too much.' (Talmon 1990: 12)

co-counselling

▷ **personal therapy, self-awareness**

Co-counselling is a formal system of reciprocal peer counselling, in which two people agree to meet and divide a session in two halves so that each spends half the time in the client role and half in the counsellor role. It is intended primarily as a personal development activity rather than a forum for addressing deeper and more complex problems, which would be better dealt with in personal therapy.

Training in co-counselling is generally based on humanistic principles and emphasises the responsibility of the partner in the client role for deciding what they want to explore and how they use their half of the time. The person in the counsellor role is expected to focus on conveying the core qualities of empathy, acceptance and genuineness, and to give the client their full attention during their allocated time. It is seen as important that this division of roles over time is adhered to and that the session does not degenerate into a two-way discussion. (This is perhaps most challenging when the counsellor and client have shared issues or experiences.)

The experience of co-counselling is rather different from that of being a counsellor and client in a skills training group in that it takes place in private, is confidential, and is intended primarily for personal development rather than skills practice. It does, however, offer useful experience as a client and raises some interesting questions about the boundaries of the counsellor–client relationship.

Some courses incorporate co-counselling as part of their programme, or as an option for students to experience. Some students may decide to experiment with it under their own initiative. Peer counselling networks based on similar principles have been adopted within some organisations as a strategy for staff support and development, and networks exist across communities that provide training and opportunities to engage in co-counselling. (See for example http://www.londoncocounselling.fsnet.co.uk/)

complaints about the course

▷ **assertiveness, distressed**

Hopefully, your experience of training will be a positive one, your needs will be met, and you will be treated fairly throughout. However, it is also possible that you will feel that this has not been the case – that you have not been supported adequately either academically or personally; that you have been discriminated against in some way or otherwise treated unjustly; that some aspect of the course has not come up to the appropriate standards; or that the tutors, administrators or someone else have not fulfilled their responsibilities appropriately. In such a case you may wish to make a complaint.

Courses should have established and explicit complaints procedures that detail how you can go about making a complaint and how it should be resolved. You should have access to the complaints procedure either in your course handbook or other documentation, or via the training institution's website. Complaints procedures generally involve beginning at a relatively informal level, bringing your complaint to the attention of an appropriately responsible person (perhaps a tutor or the course leader).

It is generally better for all concerned if complaints can be resolved at the lowest level possible, so try to be clear about what you are unhappy about, and what a satisfactory resolution would look like (see Assertiveness). It may be helpful to check with peers to see if they share your viewpoint and feel your complaint is reasonable, but you have a right to complain even if you are the only one who feels aggrieved.

If your complaint cannot be resolved at an informal level, it will need to progress to a more formal stage, when it is likely to be reviewed by a head of department or a complaints panel. This will generally involve you in preparing a case more formally, and providing evidence to support your complaint.

Depending on the institution, there may be more than one level to which you can take a complaint.

At whatever level, a judgement will need to be made about whether your complaint is valid, and, if it is, what needs to be done about it. Again, it is likely to be helpful if you have given some thought to what a satisfactory resolution would involve. You might need to challenge yourself at this stage to balance being determined against being realistic, to avoid seeking satisfaction inappropriately through revenge or punishment (though sometimes disciplinary measures may be indicated), and to consider if it is possible to achieve a 'win–win' outcome.

Training institutions are generally keen to resolve complaints internally, but if you remain dissatisfied after internal procedures have been exhausted you may still have recourse to the law, depending on the nature of your complaint. In this case you should probably seek advice from a legal professional.

If your course is BACP accredited you can also make a complaint to the BACP at any stage. The BACP complaints procedure can be found on their website.

contact time with tutors

▷ **tutors**

core model

▷ **choosing a counselling orientation, choosing a course, developing your own model of counselling, integration, values**

Counsellor training courses will generally have a 'core model', i.e. a coherent counselling model which is the basis of the training provided, and which you will be deemed to have achieved some level of competence in if you complete your training successfully. This is likely to be either a single counselling approach, such as person-centred therapy or existential therapy, or an integrative model, such as Egan's Skilled Helper Model.

Horton (2006a) notes that it is difficult to be precise about what a counselling model actually consists of, but suggests the following four elements as being either explicit or implicit in most models:

1 Basic assumptions or philosophy, including assumptions about people and assumptions about the nature and purpose of therapy.
2 Formal theory of human personality and development.
3 Clinical theory defining the goals, principles and processes of change.
4 The related therapeutic operations, skills and techniques.

You will probably have been aware of the core model for your training programme from the start – indeed this should be an important factor in choosing a course – and you may find it helpful as you progress to analyse the model you are learning in terms of these four elements. This is a useful way to check how well you understand the model at different levels, and to explore the relationships within the model between espoused theory and clinical practice. Not all models necessarily contain all of these elements and Egan's Skilled Helper Model explicitly avoids stating any formal theory of human personality and development, as the intention behind the model is to provide a framework within which a range of theoretical positions can be applied as appropriate to the needs of the client. Indeed, the intention behind open-systems models is also to be open to the integration of a range of techniques, although commonly such models do identify core skills that are central to the model.

The core model will inform much of the structure and ethos of your course. Philosophical assumptions about counselling often have some relevance to education, and it is likely that the course will attempt to embody these principles, with tutors modelling the espoused qualities of the approach etc. Thus a person-centred course is likely to have more experiential work and less didactic teaching; a psychodynamic course may place more emphasis on the case study as a learning tool; and a course based around the Egan model will encourage personal goal setting and action planning.

Most courses that are based on a single theoretical model will also include some coverage of other approaches, enabling you to compare and contrast these with the core model. Given that research into what works in counselling shows little evidence favouring one model over another for effectiveness, except in the case of some very specific client issues (Hubble et al. 1999; Cooper 2008), it is perhaps most useful for you to approach such comparisons from the point of view of what the approaches have in common, particularly in terms of how they are experienced by the client.

counselling and coaching

> ▷ choosing a career, strengths

Counselling and coaching overlap considerably, but a difference for one sub-group of coaches – executive coaches – is that they need experience in the business world, need to speak the 'language' of that world (though that language seems all too widespread to some people, so that may not be an obstacle). Jenny Rogers (2008) provides a clear and practical overview of coaching. You may find a coaching course more appealing than a counselling or psychotherapy one.

counselling and psychotherapy

> ▷ choosing a career, strengths

Many have tried to find a difference between counselling and psychotherapy, an effort Thorne long ago called a 'dismal quest' (1992: 246), and no one has found a generally accepted difference. Indeed, the terms 'counselling' and 'psychotherapy' are often used interchangeably.

Our view is that there are no significant differences between counselling and psychotherapy in depth, duration, theories and methods used, or in goals sought by the clients. For thoughtful analyses, see e.g. Thorne (1992), Feltham (1995) and McLeod (2003a). We touch on it here only because whether a course is called 'counselling' or 'psychotherapy' may affect your decision to apply for it.

You may also find another of Thorne's conclusions helpful. It has, like much of the rest of his paper, a contemporary feel. He is discussing the motives underlying the quest for differences: 'We are talking about prestige, about professional power, about livelihoods, about earning capacity, about survival of the fittest in the jungle of market forces and in the insane environment of the accountability, quality control, value for money, citizen's charter culture that we have somehow permitted to engulf us' (1992: 246).

critical thinking

> decisions, evidence-based practice, research, sleep

'Critical thinking' is a term widely and approvingly used in UK education and often taken for granted. It can sound negative and attacking but is, we think, a useful and predominantly positive meaning that distinguishes between eight aspects, which are expressed here as guidelines (Wade and Tavris 2003):

1 Ask questions and be willing to wonder.
2 Define the problem.
3 Examine the evidence.
4 Analyse assumptions and biases.
5 Avoid emotional reasoning.
6 Don't oversimplify.
7 Consider other interpretations.
8 Tolerate uncertainty.

Guideline 6 may be the key; all the others can be seen as ways of avoiding being too simple. In guideline 3, a central issue is what counts as good evidence (see entry on Evidence-based practice).

In their discussion of guideline 5, Wade and Tavris argue that clear thinking and clear feeling complement each other, that each can be dangerous in isolation. This meaning of critical thinking can also be seen as consistent with integrative counselling and therefore not as alien to counsellors and counsellor training as it first sounds. It emphasises exploration, reflection, autonomy, challenging more and drawing sound conclusions.

Weiten (2007) illustrated a more complex taxonomy of 38 skills, organised in five categories, throughout his book. The categories are: verbal reasoning skills, arguments/persuasion/analysis skills, skills in thinking as hypothesis testing, skills in working with likelihood and uncertainty, and decision-making and problem-solving skills. Another recent and more manageable attempt, which overlaps with Wade and Tavris's, was made by Bensley (2008), who suggested seven strategies:

1 Strive for precision and clarity in your thinking.
2 Seek reasons.
3 Examine alternative viewpoints fairly.
4 Be sensitive to the quality of evidence.
5 Consider how much evidence is available.
6 Draw conclusions consistent with the best evidence available.
7 Seek feedback and reflect on the quality of your thinking.

We suggest that you compile your own list from one or more of these and other sources and that using your list will add to your counselling. However, and in the spirit of several of Wade and Tavris's guidelines, there is another view: that critical thinking is not universally valued. For example, Macfarlane (2007) discussed his experience with Japanese students in the UK and in Tokyo. They 'come from a tradition that places a high value on memory, conformity to great masters and accuracy in detail' (p. 14). His postgraduate students 'sat quietly and refused to express opinions of disagreement or even ask questions'. Thus, harmony was valued much more than debate or confrontation. Moreover, 'if two ideas clash or contradict each other according to strict logic, that can be overlooked, for reason is fallible and inferior to emotion and intuition' (p. 14).

Returning to the UK perspective, Feltham (1996) argued for a 'specific critical component' at the heart of counsellor training (pp. 297–8) and gave several examples. Thus, he wondered if the core theoretical model is 'a myth born out of the anxieties of professionalisation and failure to apply tests of logic and efficacy' (p. 299); inquired into the reality and limits of confidentiality; suggested that lifelong regular supervision may not actually be essential for professionalism or effectiveness; and speculated that some boundaries should be flexible and that counsellor training may be unnecessary, and, for some people, counter-productive.

criticisms of counselling, and replies

> ▷ assertiveness, critical thinking, evidence-based practice, motives, relationships with friends, family and work colleagues

In the last few years, counselling has had much more (broadly) good publicity, in newspapers and TV news programmes and in dramas (e.g. *The Sopranos*), than bad. This seems both to reflect a greater general acceptance of its value and to contribute to that acceptance. However, there have also been some strongly expressed criticisms, and trainee counsellors may be confronted with these. We first discuss three aspects of replying to criticisms and then some examples of those criticisms. The three aspects are evidence of the effectiveness of counselling, the strategy of listening and judging whether or not to reply.

The effectiveness of counselling

It is now clearly established that counselling is effective (Lambert 2004; Cooper 2008). It works for a wide range of problems and clients. On the other hand, relatively little is known about *why* it works, with factors common to the various orientations, e.g. empathy, repair of 'alliance ruptures', a collaborative approach and client readiness to change, perhaps the most likely explanations (Hubble et al. 1999; Cooper 2008). Moreover, counselling is occasionally harmful and many of the outcome measures are self-reported (not always a weakness in itself but more variety would be stronger), and follow-up periods are usually a year at most.

One or two specific examples of research on effectiveness will strengthen this kind of rejoinder, but we think it's best to choose these yourself. The tone with which you use them is important: mostly calm and rational, with a subtext of 'There's a lot of rigorous research on this, literally hundreds of studies, and good though not universal agreement among researchers.'

A second general reply

Another option is to listen hard to the person attacking or challenging counselling (and directly or indirectly you). This may not be easy especially if you feel threatened, but it is good practice! Your listening can be empathic, disputing or both. Thus, you can say for example, 'You're very angry about ...' (an empathic response), or 'That's a shocking story. How do you know it's true or not exaggerated?' or 'That seems to me a sweeping statement. What's your evidence for it?' (two disputing responses).

If the discussion continues, you might find it helpful to say that counsellors vary in effectiveness and in how ethical they are (just as the police, doctors etc. vary), and that the evidence generally – from thousands of studies, some of them very large-scale and rigorous – is that most counsellors are effective and ethical.

A third option

Some criticisms and critics aren't worth replying to: yesterday's news.

Some critiques

This section is intended to provide a starting point for understanding and replying to some of the main criticisms, learning where they're flawed and where they may have a point. The criticisms we briefly summarise and comment on are from Morrall (2008), Furedi (2003) and Masson (1989). These are more attacks than critiques. There are also two other kinds of critique: those by counsellors of one approach to counselling or psychotherapy about other approaches (e.g. Lazarus in Dryden 1991), and those also from within counselling, but taking a constructive tone (e.g. Feltham 1996).

Morrall (2008)

Morrall takes a sociological perspective, which he sees as 'causing trouble', by 'asking lots of challenging questions about what are otherwise taken-for-granted ideas, values and social edifices' (p. 2). That appeals to us (they are core academic values) but his emotive language less so, though it has entertaining moments.

For example, Morrall writes about 'the absurdly constricted and naïve nature of therapy' and its 'reckless lack of concern about (global) society' (p. 3) – for example, about the role of poverty in human suffering. This is the claim, made by others too, e.g. Smail, Furedi, that therapy encourages us to believe that the causes of our problems and distress lie within ourselves rather than from social and economic inequalities. It then aims to help us change ourselves rather than trying to change those 'inequalities' (a too gentle term).

Our view is that therapy (counselling) has limitations and that some counsellors should be more modest in their claims, and we agree that society is a major cause of distress. But it's not the only cause and we do contribute to our own distress too. Moreover, counselling aims to free people (at least to some extent) from those internal causes to become more authentic, and some former clients will express themselves politically more, and we expect more effectively, than they would have done without their experience of counselling.

Morrall is open about his own experiences of counsellor training and relationship therapy. He seems to us to have been very unlucky in his therapists (taking his accounts at face value); no wonder he was mystified and angry. He does say that he hopes his experiences of therapy were 'idiosyncratic'. We hope (and think) so too!

Two key sentences in Morrall's Introduction are: 'Too much time and energy is spent on the minutiae of institutional and personal agendas, rather than on what really matters. What really matters is tackling directly and virulently human suffering and social injustice *globally*' (his emphasis, p. 6). Thus he wants all of us to be radical sociologists like him. And he accuses therapy of being 'dysfunctional; arrogant; selfish; abusive; infectious; insane; and deceitful' (p. 8), with a chapter on each charge.

We see this critique as lively and deeply felt but misguided. The world needs some radical sociologists and political activists and it needs some good counsellors, as well as many other kinds of people. It needs those who study people at different levels of analysis, from neuropsychology to economics. However, this is a detailed set of critiques which may well deserve a detailed reply, and Morrall does also add, perhaps rather grudgingly, that some therapists may enlighten sociology too.

Furedi (2003)

Furedi argues that experiences that are normal parts of life, e.g. loss, depression, stress, disappointment, have been pathologised: redefined as problems which need to be cured. The causes of this shift include the decline of religion and community spirit. In their place are, among others, 'a whole army of counsellors'. He sees this shift as sinister because it encourages dependency and a victim mentality, and directs anger, which should be with the state, to personal issues.

Like Morrall, Furedi is a sociologist and there is *some* truth in his view (we think). In particular, there does seem to be a modern tendency to turn normal life events into medical problems. However, Furedi seems too lacking in compassion, too strident and too extreme; his philosophy too much that of the rugged individualist: sink or swim, pull yourself together. Because counselling can encourage dependency, it doesn't mean that it inevitably does. On the contrary, it much more often encourages autonomy and self-awareness, and helps people recover from being victims.

Masson (1989)

Masson's main argument is that all psychotherapists exploit their clients: the 'very idea' of psychotherapy – any form of it – is wrong: 'The structure of psychotherapy is such that no matter how kindly a person is, when that person becomes a therapist, he or she is engaged in acts that are bound to diminish the dignity, autonomy, and freedom of the person who comes for help' (p. 24).

Masson's evidence, however, is anecdotal. The anecdotes are vividly described and shocking, and many of the abuses were covered up by colleagues, but generalising to all or many therapists is not justified. The valid aspect of his argument is that the therapeutic relationship is intrinsically unequal – perhaps even in co-counselling – but this does not inevitably or usually lead to abuse and exploitation. The research on effectiveness is strong evidence that it does not, and that at the heart of therapy, most of the time, is real empathy and compassion.

d

decisions, making

▷ assertiveness, critical thinking, journal, self-awareness, strengths, values, writing (expressive)

Several other entries are relevant to making better decisions, for example those on Assertiveness, Values and Strengths. Three ways of deciding are outlined below, followed by some variations and refinements. For some decisions and people, one of the methods will fit better. For other decisions, you may wish to try more than one method.

The *first method* is the simplest. It assumes that some people make good decisions by listing the points or arguments for and against, then perhaps giving each argument a weighting, while others decide best by how they 'feel' (also known as 'gut instinct'). The feeling may be immediate or develop gradually in strength. The feeling way of deciding recognises that emotions are at least as important as logic because they help identify what we care and don't care (care less) about. The best decisions may come from using both processes, but if one seems more natural to you, we suggest emphasising that one the most.

The *second method* is an elaboration of the first, in four stages:

1 What are the relevant facts or details? e.g. What was actually said? *How* did it seem to be said?

2 What are all the possible (however unlikely) ways of looking at these facts? Are any theories or models relevant? Are any decisions I've made in similar situations relevant?

3 What is the most logical decision? What are the short- and long-term consequences of each choice likely to be? What are the pros and cons? What 'makes sense'?

4 What are the probable effects on other people? Which choice is most in tune with my values? Which feels most 'right'?

The stages can be used in *any* order, e.g. some people tend to imagine lots of possibilities before checking the facts (or indeed without checking the facts, though if any of the stages is missed out, this is likely to reduce the quality of the decision).

According to psychological type theory (Bayne 2004), which underlies the first two methods, each of us is likely to favour one or two of the stages and therefore to neglect the others. If we do, the following outcomes become more likely:

Neglect or miss out	Likely effect
Stage 1	Unforeseen practical difficulties
Stage 2	Another decision would have been better
Stage 3	Unexpected and unpleasant consequences
Stage 4	The decision upsets you or others

Type theory also suggests that it can be very useful to consult someone with different strengths to your own for their views. For example, if you're most at home with stages 2 and 4, consult someone who more naturally emphasises 1 and 3. There is good evidence for the basic theory (Bayne 2005) but no research so far on its application to making decisions.

The *third method* of deciding is a technique from Gestalt therapy: two-chair technique. The person with a decision literally sits alternately in two chairs, expressing the arguments for a decision in one chair and the arguments against in the other. This technique can also be done on paper. There is some well-designed research on the effectiveness of two-chair technique (Clarke and Greenberg 1986; Elliott et al. 2004), but no comparisons of the effectiveness of using paper versus actual chairs as yet.

Refinements and variations of the first two methods of deciding include:

1 Sleep on it.
2 Use the exercise on rights in the entry on Assertiveness.
3 Consider the skill of saying no in the same entry, e.g. is a trial run possible?
4 Work on your self-awareness, e.g. of your values.
5 Toss a coin or ask someone else to decide. Your reaction to the result may clarify your decision.
6 Sometimes, not making a decision is the best option.
7 Visualise each outcome.
8 Write about it in the way suggested in the entry on the Journal.

deferring

▷ decisions, stress

In academic terms, to defer means to put something off, usually through a fairly formal process, to an agreed date later than that which was originally specified. The term is usually used in relation to starting a course, submitting an assessment or gaining an award. For example, if you've been offered a place to start a course at a particular time, but changes to your personal circumstances make that difficult, it may be possible to defer your entry to the course until the next available start date, by which time you might hope to have settled into a new job, negotiated study time with your employer, or recovered from an illness.

Similarly, if personal or health difficulties are preventing you from completing an assessment by the due date, it may be possible to *defer* submission to an agreed later date. You should note, however, that current trends within the education sector are making this increasingly difficult. In recent years academic regulations have tended to become tighter around extensions to submission dates, to the extent that in some institutions there is no longer any possibility of deferring submission. If you are unable to meet the specified date you may be deemed to have used one of your available opportunities to pass the assessment in question and have to move to a resubmission at the date specified for that. You should check your course regulations carefully in relation to submission dates, resubmission opportunities, policies on extenuating circumstances etc.

If for some reason you have not completed all of the course requirements by the official end of the course you may find that your award is *deferred* until you have done so. In counsellor training courses, the most likely reason for this is probably that you need to do more counselling hours. BACP accredited training programmes are required to include a supervised practice placement of at least 100 hours client work (that's the 2009 figure but it will rise to 150 hours soon), and it is not uncommon for students to find it difficult to secure a placement and complete the required hours in time. There is usually a procedure in place to account for this, and again you should check the course regulations to be clear about what happens if you have not completed your hours by the end of the course, how much additional time you can have to complete, and what arrangements are in place for support and supervision while you do so.

de-skilled, feeling

▷ expectations of training, good counsellors, self-esteem, skills training, stress

developing your own model of counselling

▷ choosing a counselling orientation, core model, critical thinking, integration, metaphors, motives, self-esteem, values

As you develop and gain experience as a counsellor it is likely that your practice will evolve in ways which are unique and personal to you. While you are still in training there will probably be some requirement that you adhere to the values of your course's core model, show that you understand and can apply its theoretical concepts and can demonstrate competence in its core skills and techniques, but within these boundaries it is almost inevitable that individual students will be developing in different ways.

It is interesting and useful to observe those variations in style and application in your peers, and we would encourage you to do this in a reflective and critical way (in the positive sense of critical). This is valuable both in enabling you to give constructive critical feedback to your peers, and in encouraging you to think carefully about what you can take from the range of available role models (peers, tutors, video recordings etc.) for your own development.

Some integrative training courses actively encourage students to be aware of, and focus on their own development of, a unique personal style (or, in time, model) and may ask you to describe and discuss it in an assessment task. The current BACP process for individual accreditation as a counsellor or psychotherapist includes the requirement that you write a personal rationale for your practice which includes reference to a coherent theoretical framework (which can be a recognised model or your own personal integration) and that you write about work with one or two clients as an illustration of this in practice.

A high proportion of UK practitioners describe themselves as integrative or eclectic, in spite of the fact that the majority of training courses still have a single theoretical model as their core. This strongly suggests that with experience many counsellors are developing their own model and diverging from the model in which they gained their initial training (Horton 2006b).

Skovholt and Ronnestad (1995) note that most experienced therapists will be less concerned with the more abstract aspects of theory and more concerned with issues of theory, process and technique, which are more closely linked to clinical practice. You may therefore find that as you develop your own model, it tends to be focused on clinical theory and therapeutic operations rather than basic assumptions and formal theory. You may find that Horton's (2006a) four elements of a counselling model, outlined in the Core model entry above, form a useful template for examining your own developing model.

Describing your own model in terms of these elements can be a useful exercise as you near the end of your training course, and worth repeating at intervals as you gain experience and develop. A particularly interesting area to reflect upon is the extent to which what you see as your basic assumptions and formal theory continue to be reflected in how you actually work with clients. It is not uncommon to find that one's practice has evolved in ways which incorporate a wider range of approaches or techniques than might be expected to fit in with espoused assumptions and theories. If this happens, it is a valuable opportunity for you to challenge your assumptions and refine your position (either by making your personal model more explicit, or by working on reasserting your core values/assumptions/theory in your practice).

disability

▷ imagery, multiculturalism

If you have a disability you have a right to expect not to be discriminated against because of it and, as a student, you have a right to expect a learning experience comparable to that of your peers. In the UK, the Disability Discrimination Act (DDA) 1995 and the revised act of 2005 (see: http://www.opsi.gov.uk/acts/acts2005/ukpga_20050013_en_1) defines a disabled person as one who 'has a physical or mental impairment which has a substantial and long-term adverse effect upon his [*sic*] ability to carry out normal day-to-day activities'. It establishes the rights of those with disabilities, and sets out responsibilities for institutions (including education providers) to promote equality and inclusiveness and avoid discrimination. In practice this can mean that you have access to appropriate support and resources to enable you to undertake the course, and that learning and teaching and assessment methods should not disadvantage you with respect to other students.

Institutions are expected to take reasonable steps to find out if a person is disabled, but if you have a disability it is likely to be in your interests to make the training institution aware of this at the earliest opportunity and discuss your needs in detail, so that appropriate arrangements can be put in place. This is particularly important in relation to assessment as, depending on the nature of your disability, special or alternative arrangements for assessment may need to be developed.

Further information regarding the DDA, its implications for education providers and the rights of disabled students can be found at the following websites:

> http://www.open.ac.uk/inclusiveteaching/pages/legal-and-
> professional-requirements/disability-discrimination-act-part-4.php
> http://www.qaa.ac.uk/academicinfrastructure/codeOfPractice/
> section3/default.asp
> http://www.equalityhumanrights.com/your-rights/rights-in-different-
> settings/learning-and-training/

discouraged, feeling

> ▷ distressed

distressed, feeling

> ▷ complaints about a course, expectations, failing, fears, loss, personal development, personal therapy, rejection, relationships, self-awareness, self-esteem, stress

Counsellor training presents some unusual challenges to students, particularly in terms of the emphasis placed on self-awareness and personal development, and many aspects of your course have the potential to lead to distress. Examples might be conflict within the group, getting in touch with difficult personal issues during classroom sessions or skills practice, a difficult session with a client, 'fallout' from the course into relationships with family and friends, or individual 'triggers' which might be set off by a discussion topic, by feedback from a peer, client or tutor, or by personal reflection.

The term 'distress' applies when the impact on you is emotionally painful to the extent that it seems to exceed your capacity to cope. This can be a short-lived experience which reverts, after some 'breathing space' or support, back to a stress which is within your coping resources. However, in some cases, particularly if distress is not fully acknowledged and addressed, it can last longer and have more serious consequences.

If you feel distressed during your counselling training, the first step is to recognise it for what it is and acknowledge it to yourself. You are then in a position to consider your immediate needs. Often we have found that the most beneficial course of action is to acknowledge it as openly as you feel able to. Depending on the nature of your course, your levels of trust and confidence, and the specific impact the distress is having on you, this might mean sharing it with your group, with a trusted peer, or with a tutor. In any case, try to avoid the temptation to minimise your distress and be as congruent as you can be about how you feel and what kind of support you need. Sometimes you may find that you are encouraged to 'stay with' your distress in order to work through it. We have often seen the benefits of this approach and sometimes issues can be resolved or ameliorated quite quickly, but you should not feel bullied or intimidated into doing so if you are sure that a different approach is what you need in order to cope.

Feeling distressed may indicate that you would benefit from additional support of some kind, or that problems have surfaced which are ready to be addressed. It can be useful to discuss this with your tutor. You may find that personal therapy or other coping resources seem appropriate. On a positive note, our experience has been that most distress is a signal of an unmet need, and represents an opportunity to confront that need or an underlying problem and deal with it. It is unfortunate that this is a process that involves a degree of pain, but the function of that pain seems similar to that of physical pain – to highlight a problem that needs attention and that could cause further distress if not dealt with.

diversity

> disability, gender, imagery, multiculturalism, personality theory, psychological type, sexual orientation

As a counsellor you will find yourself working with clients who are different from you in many ways. Forming a therapeutic relationship is challenging and differences in worldviews, values etc. can make it more so. Thus, your personal history, family background, language, gender, sexuality, ethnicity, spirituality, age, socioeconomic status etc. will affect your counselling and you need to be aware of your own biases, values, expectations and personal agenda, otherwise you risk projecting them onto clients or are likely to distort your understanding of your clients' worldviews or experiences.

The following exercise is a starting point for preparing yourself to work with diverse clients:

1 Make a list of factors which you feel describe your own 'personal culture', and which have shaped your values, beliefs, attitudes, worldview etc. Begin with the obvious such as gender, ethnicity, socioeconomic status, sexuality etc. but consider other factors related to family and family traditions/assumptions, sub-groups, peer groups, political affiliations, significant life experiences and choices which have shaped your self-concept, beliefs, attitudes and values.
   ‣ Also make a list of people (family and other relationships) who you can identify as having influenced your beliefs/attitudes/values/sense of who you are, etc.
   ‣ What messages have you received from any groups to which you see yourself as belonging relating to values, behaviours, expectations, lifestyle, family relationships, gender roles, education, politics etc.?
2 Consider which elements on your lists you see as most positive and you feel good about, and also whether there are any factors which you feel less comfortable with, or which may have a 'shadow side'. Consider to what extent there are factors that come into conflict with each other.
3 If you can find a peer or colleague willing to share in this exercise, take turns sharing as much of this as you feel comfortable with. The purpose at this stage is to enable each of you to gain as full a picture as you can of the 'personal culture' of the other, raising awareness of aspects you might have in common and areas of difference. Discuss the challenges that would be involved in gaining a deeper understanding of each other's experience and worldview.
4 Consider how your personal culture might influence your counselling (both positively and negatively) in terms of expectations, attitudes, values, potential biases etc. and your ability to form effective therapeutic alliances with diverse clients.
5 Try to identify at least one goal for yourself related to working in a way which is sensitive to difference and diversity.

dropping out of your course

▷ assertiveness, decisions, deferring, failing, loss, strengths, stress

You may be faced with a choice between continuing with your course when it doesn't feel right or there are other problems, and dropping out. There's a tendency, in education and in government, to see continuing a course as 'good' and dropping out as 'failure'. This seems to us to be a wrong distinction: sometimes the course isn't right for a student, or not right at this time, and it's therefore better in every respect except retention figures for the student to drop out or defer.

As long as the decision to leave is a good one, the student, the other students on their course, the tutors, and the college or university, all benefit. However, students do sometimes leave for insufficient reasons and (not surprisingly) we suggest exploring and reflecting on what's 'going on', consulting with fellow students, tutors and others (the entries on Assertiveness skills and Decisions may be useful here), considering alternative strategies (Critical thinking) and being appropriately positive (e.g. if counselling – all forms – isn't right for you, does this imply anything about your strengths and therefore, assuming a strength-based approach is valid, what *is* right for you?). Dropping out can be a positive decision, or have positive elements.

d

e

effectiveness of counselling

▷ criticisms of counselling, evidence-based practice, future of counselling, integrative counselling

effectiveness of counsellor training

▷ evidence-based practice, good counsellors, personal therapy, relationships with friends

There has been only a little research so far on the impact of counsellor education and training (Dryden and Feltham 1994; McLeod 2003a). McLeod (2003a) sees this lack as partly due to the history of counsellor training. There are several examples of research on effectiveness in this book, e.g. in the entry on Relationships with friends, and some elements of counsellor training have been studied sufficiently to justify research reviews, for example skills training (Hill and Lent 2006) and personal therapy (Norcross 2005).

ending of your course

▷ loss

Counsellors need to be able to manage endings effectively in order to bring their therapeutic relationships with clients to a satisfactory close – facing the reality of the ending, celebrating what has been achieved, acknowledging and experiencing feelings about the end of the relationship, preparing for a new stage in life, and finding ways to carry forward what has been valuable. All of these can equally apply to the end of the course and of the relationship with the group, and the ending offers you an opportunity to learn more about yourself and how you respond to and manage these transitions.

You can take the chance to be aware of your experience and process it as it occurs, and work towards making it positive and fulfilling for yourself and others. Notice what you feel, what thoughts you have, what you embrace and what you are tempted to avoid, what you find difficult and what you enjoy.

The period leading up to the ending is likely to be stressful and tiring. On most courses there are a number of important assessments to complete as the end approaches, and these can feel like the biggest test. You will want to demonstrate that you have achieved the required standards and that you have earned the qualification – that you are a competent and safe practitioner.

This can add an extra level of stress to the task, and if a number of submission deadlines occur close together you may need to take particular care with planning your work, managing your time, and maintaining some balance in your life so as not to run out of energy.

There is likely to be some final assessment of your counselling qualities and skills. The format this takes varies across courses, but live demonstrations, submission of recordings with analysis/evaluation, presentations of recordings with commentary, and viva voce examinations based on recordings or case studies are all possibilities. Some stress around these assessments is probably inevitable for most students, but you can help yourself to manage it by good preparation, being clear about assessment procedures and criteria, practising or rehearsing, and reminding yourself that you are not expected to achieve a perfect performance. Indeed in many of these 'final' assessments there are opportunities to gain credit by realistically evaluating what you have done, demonstrating your awareness and ability to reflect on your performance, and making constructive comment about what you might have done differently.

Aside from all the work, it is important to stay in touch with the process of the group ending. Relationships will have been formed with peers and tutors over an extended period, and due to the nature of counsellor training and the core relationship qualities you have been working on, these relationships are likely to be closer and deeper than you might have been expecting. Time should be available to reflect on and share experiences of the ending with the group, and your tutors may provide some structured activities to facilitate this. Most groups take the opportunity to organise a social activity to celebrate the ending in a different way.

There may be a temptation to attempt to avoid or deny the ending. Some groups make plans to continue meeting, either socially, for mutual support, or for discussion, peer supervision etc. This can be positive and healthy, though in our experience it rarely involves the whole group, or continues for long. However, we feel it is important to recognise that whatever might be planned for the future, the life of the group as it currently exists – i.e. as a counsellor training course group – is ending, and so accepting that, celebrating it, experiencing the feelings associated with it, making the transition to a new stage of life and carrying the experience forward in a meaningful way are all tasks that should be addressed.

It is of course possible that you may not be finished when the course ends. Some students are likely to have client hours to complete and some may have assessments to resubmit. If you find yourself in that position, it will add additional complications to the ending process, but it is still important to attend to the ending issues as described above, before gathering your energy again to complete the process. Make sure you are aware of, and make use of, the support available during the time you are completing any outstanding tasks.

As a part of the ending, tutors are likely to want to gather evaluation data from you. This may involve filling in forms or taking part in a group evaluation. Whilst there is no direct benefit for you in this, most tutors genuinely want to keep developing and improving their courses, and they value your input. What you have most valued and why can be as useful and important as what you feel could be improved. As with all feedback, try to be constructive and realistic. Complaints about the quality of the food or the opening times of the canteen can be important and real issues, but they are largely outside of the tutors' direct control; whereas suggestions about, for example, the sequencing of sessions, learning and teaching methods used, or the type of feedback that was most valued in skills groups can be acted upon directly and can make a real difference for subsequent groups.

Given that end-of-course evaluations can only benefit subsequent course groups, they are perhaps not the best time to present a list of things you are unhappy about regarding the course. (If you think things could be done better or differently or if something isn't working for you, it might be possible to do something about it if you communicate it to the tutors as and when it becomes an issue.)

Ending the course is likely to leave you with some space in your life. This may feel like a great relief or it may feel like a gap. In either case you may wish to take the opportunity to reconnect with other aspects of your life that to some extent have probably been 'on hold' or neglected during your training. This could involve family, friends who may have felt less of your presence than usual, or leisure activities, interests and hobbies. You now have an opportunity to reinvest the energy that has been directed towards your course into other areas.

Finally, the end of your training is only really the beginning of your development as a counsellor. You may wish to consider how your client work is to develop, decide what further training or professional development you wish to undertake, make appropriate arrangements for supervision, perhaps seek paid work as a counsellor or begin private practice, and, if working towards BACP accreditation, continue to accumulate client hours and make sure you are laying the groundwork to satisfy the criteria when you submit your application.

essays and reports, writing

▷ assessments of essays and reports, critical thinking, freewriting, notes, relaxation, study skills

'Most of my work consists of crossing out. That's the secret of all good writing.' (Source unknown)

There is plenty of advice about writing essays available to students of all subjects. If you are studying at a sizeable institution, it is likely that there will be a study skills or writing skills service available, and if you haven't written an essay for a while it will probably be useful to pay a visit and see what resources and help they can offer. Alternatively, there are a number of useful texts (e.g. Levin 2004; Greetham 2008) and web resources (e.g. http://www.theory.org.uk/david/essaywriting.pdf) you can use. Most of the advice centres around how to gather the information you need, how to organise it into a logical structure, how to express yourself in an appropriate style, and how to 'do' analysis and critical thinking in your essay.

Of the many approaches to improving writing, two seem to us particularly valuable. One is based on research with academic writers, both 'blocked' and relatively successful (Boice 1994), the other on psychological type theory (Bayne 2004).

Boice's research

Boice's main findings and recommendations included:

1 Write little and often.

   Boice used the phrase 'brief, daily sessions', by which he meant 10 minutes to an hour. He found this to be much more enjoyable and effective than 'binge writing' (several hours at a time). However, all his findings and the advice that follows from them apply to writers generally and therefore they may not suit you.

2 Stop before you get tired.

3 Define writing broadly to include taking notes and organising and 'playing' with them. Indeed, give as much time to these as to what most people think of as writing. This reduces the terror of the blank page and any failure of inspiration.

4 Check your body for tension from time to time and stretch, breathe deeply etc. to relax.

5 Check your expectations and beliefs about you and writing, and about writers too. For example, most writers rewrite many times.

6 Write your first draft roughly and then turn to writing it well, i.e. revision and editing.

Psychological type theory

This theory suggests why the advice of Boice and others will suit some writers (perhaps most) and not others. It assumes we each have a natural style and aims to help us find it more quickly than the usual haphazard or well-meant – but wrong for you – trial-and-error approach. However, an element of trial and error – finding your own way – is probably inevitable.

In general terms, some of the following aspects of writing are likely to come more easily to each person than others, and the implication is to do those first and add the other aspects later:

- Breadth and variety
- Depth and selection
- Details, examples
- Critical thinking (defined broadly – see entry)
- Logical order
- Fluency
- Impact on the reader
- Conclusions

Use of 'I'

A challenging aspect of writing essays on a counselling course is often that they are not straightforward academic essays. The above advice can be valuable, but unlike for example a history student, you may also be expected to include evidence of self-awareness, reflection, self-challenge and personal development. This more personal aspect of writing essays can be difficult to balance with the academic side. The first challenge is to get the balance right in terms of proportion – how much of the essay should be devoted to demonstrating your knowledge, understanding and critical thinking, and how much to self-awareness, personal reflection etc. The assessment guidelines and criteria should give you some idea of the relative weighting of these aspects, but if in doubt ask your tutor to clarify and arrange a tutorial if necessary. Make sure that you are clear about what is required so that you gain as much as possible from the process (rather than worrying about whether you have the basic recipe right).

A second and related challenge is use of the word 'I'. Attitudes to this vary, but our view is that attempting to write about personal reflection and development sounds awkward and contrived if not written in the first person, and moving between first- and third-person styles in 'personal' and 'academic' sections of an essay can be messy. Banning it always was spurious, a pretence at being objective. If you're offering an opinion – and your thoughts, views and reactions are a vital part of a good essay or report (they should not be mere summaries of your reading) – then using 'I' is clearer and more direct.

In any case, you need to develop a style which can communicate knowledge and analysis convincingly, but which can also express some of the subtleties of your inner processes in a congruent way. You may find it helpful to get someone to look over a sample section of your work to give you some feedback on the style and how it comes across to a reader. Your tutors may be willing to do this in a tutorial, or a writing skills tutor may be available, but you may also have a friend or family member who is capable of providing some useful feedback.

Other advice

Some ideas that work for one or both of us or that we have seen work for others:

- When editing, ask of each word or phrase, 'Does it need to be here?' What happens if you delete it?
- Regard writing as a way of clarifying what you think and feel. It can be an act of discovery.
- Begin with a summary/overview.
- Bear in mind that sometimes a later – or the last – paragraph of a draft is a good first paragraph.
- Read what you've written aloud.

ethics, professional

▷ **boundaries, critical thinking, decisions**

Ethical dilemmas present a challenge to all counsellors, but they can be a particular source of anxiety or stress early in your development when you have relatively little experience of managing and resolving them. Questions like 'What do I do if a client expresses suicidal intentions but won't seek any help apart from me?' or 'What if a client who has been sexually abused by a family member tells me that person is now caring for other young children?' can prey on your mind and be very frightening. Fortunately, you will rarely have to make such complex decisions unsupported except in a crisis, and even then most counselling agencies have developed policies for such situations. (Obviously you should familiarise yourself with these.)

For most dilemmas you will find that the combination of the BACP Ethical Framework (BACP, 2009b) – or other code of ethics if appropriate – and discussion in supervision will enable you to work out what to do. Unlike the previous BACP 'Code of Ethics and Practice' and some other professional codes, the current ethical framework focuses more on providing guidance on *how* to resolve an ethical dilemma, rather than a series of 'dos' and 'don'ts' that tell you *what* you should do. It describes the values and personal qualities seen as important in relation to ethical practice, but perhaps most usefully for trainees, provides a set of six ethical principles which you should apply when deciding how to act in response to a dilemma. These are:

- *Fidelity*: Honour the trust placed in you by the client by staying with agreements and contracts you have made.
- *Autonomy*: Respect the client's right to make his or her own decisions.
- *Beneficence*: Act in ways most likely to promote the client's well-being.
- *Non-maleficence*: Act in ways most likely to avoid harm to the client (or others).
- *Justice*: Be fair to the client and take account of legal requirements and obligations.
- *Self-respect*: Pay attention to your own needs and welfare.

The process of working through an ethical dilemma then involves analysing it carefully (What exactly is the dilemma? Whose dilemma is it? What are the potential undesired outcomes to be avoided?); generating a list of options for action and considering their possible consequences; and weighing these options in terms of the above ethical principles. It is unlikely that all of the ethical principles will point towards the same course of action; for example, the course of action most likely to benefit the client (the beneficence principle) may involve some risk and could go wrong (the non-maleficence principle), so you will also need to consider which principles have priority in any given situation. (It might be argued, for example, that non-maleficence and justice often represent an ethical 'bottom line' in crisis situations.) For an inexperienced counsellor, this process is best worked through with your supervisor, and most supervisors are willing to provide you with a means of contacting them for consultation in a crisis. In some situations you may also need to be aware of the legal situation (e.g. child protection legislation) or seek legal advice.

Probably the most important thing for an inexperienced counsellor is not to avoid or deny ethical dilemmas – pretending they are not there is unlikely to lead to them going away, and could well make things worse. If you feel uncomfortable or awkward about your work with a particular client, reflect on it and discuss it in supervision to see if there is an ethical dilemma lurking somewhere, and address it.

evidence-based practice (EBP)

> ▷ clinical wisdom, critical thinking, criticisms, ethics, reading

Evidence-based practice is an influential trend in many professions including counselling.

It has strengths but also problems (Wessely 2001; Bayne et al. 2008). For example, evidence doesn't exist yet on many aspects of counsellor training and counselling, and where the evidence does exist it is often seriously flawed, e.g. through publication bias (when only 'positive' results have been published and numerous 'negative' results have been filed), or through over-interpretation of one or two studies.

This is to recognise the nature of science, and the number and complexity of the issues, *not* to take an anti-science or anti-evidence position. On the contrary, counsellors and trainee counsellors have an ethical and legal responsibility to be up to date with relevant research and to make defensible inferences that inform our strategies with our clients. While it's obviously not practical to read all the relevant literature on most issues, reading some expert summaries, e.g. Cooper (2008) and the BACP series of scoping reviews, is possible and a desirable part of being a counsellor.

exercise, physical

▷ relaxation

We see you looking after yourself physically as a professional responsibility for counsellors, and the evidence for the benefits of physical exercise for people in general is very strong (Taylor 2009). However, some people have no wish to exercise for at least 30 minutes of 'low intensity' activity per day as recommended in government guidelines, and some seem to survive well without exercise. The rest of this entry is for those who wish to exercise more.

Walking is a good example of a low intensity activity and pedometers, which are readily available, have been found to increase the amount many people walk. The goal of walking 10,000 steps a day (3–5 miles) has been widely publicised. It also introduces a period for reflection – though for some of us it's boring and there are other problems too, e.g. chafing, hostile dogs and lightning. Standard advice on these is Vaseline; face it and talk calmly but if its tail is held high and it's stiff, it's about to attack and you must fend it off as best you can; and squat in an open space as low as you can, respectively!

For advice on walking, running and other exercise see Bradley (2007), Glover and Shepherd (1996), Schlosberg and Neporent (2005), Whalley and Jackson (2008) and the website runnersworld.com. The advice can be very sophisticated, e.g. gait analysis from a specialist physiotherapist, and choosing appropriate shoes for the activity and for you. However, the main general principles are to become more active *gradually and comfortably* in ways that you enjoy, and to have rest days.

When you can gradually and comfortably exercise for a total of 30 minutes most days (five out of seven), that may be enough for you. However, the 2008 British Association of Sport and Exercise Sciences (Bases) guidelines recommends 'vigorous exercise' two or three times a week as a healthier alternative. They define 'vigorous' as a session in which it's difficult to speak in sentences, and which lasts several minutes – much more demanding!

exercises, experiential

▷ assertiveness, critical thinking, imagery, self-awareness

Most counselling courses will have 'workshops' as their main mode of teaching. Depending to some extent on how well they are run, workshops appeal to some trainees much more than others. For some, it's so much better to be doing something and in particular *experiencing* ideas, attitudes and behaviour than it is to be told about them. For others, listening to a lecture (or not listening) is how they prefer to learn – or it may just feel safer.

As a trainee, you have considerable influence on the effectiveness of experiential exercises. First, you can try to suspend any disbelief you have about the exercise and take part in it as fully as you feel comfortable with. Second, you can report your reactions openly or be open about not reporting them.

Reflection is an important aspect of *learning* from experience (rather than just accumulating experience in an uncritical way). If you'd like the analysis and discussion of an exercise to be more in-depth, you can structure it, either for yourself or as a suggestion to the tutor, for example one or more of the following aspects:

> - What happened (if the exercise was an activity)?
> - What do you think and feel about what happened during the exercise?
> - Are there possible implications for you, for other people and for counselling?
> - Are there implications for a theory, model or concept?
> - Are there ways the exercise might be improved?

exhausted, feeling

> ▷ expectations, fears, relaxation, sleep, stress

expectations of training

> ▷ brochures, choosing a course, distressed, fears, metaphors, relationships with friends etc., trust

Counsellor training is likely to involve a lot of hard work, difficult learning, and personal challenges. If you are aware of that before you start then it is likely that you have made the decision to do it because you have high expectations about what the experience will be like. And indeed for many students it is a positive experience that is both life changing and life enhancing. However, it is not without its costs and it helps to have realistic expectations about the process.

For most students there are times when feeling tired or exhausted, facing up to developing self-knowledge, trying to relate to others with empathy, acceptance and genuineness, managing your emotional responses to the issues raised, keeping on top of reading, journal writing, professional logs etc. can feel overwhelming. The common experience of feeling de-skilled early in training can be very discouraging ('I used to think I could do this quite well but now I can't even seem to get the basics right'). Personal relationships are likely to suffer when much of your energy is needed for your training, and you may find that significant others do not always respond positively to the changes they perceive in you.

If you are aware that problems like these are likely to occur then to some extent you can prepare for them – think about what support you will need and how you will get it, how you will manage your time effectively, and how you will maintain some balance in your life to keep yourself and your significant relationships healthy. Aside from the time to attend the course, you also need to factor in time to read, reflect and work on assignments, and time to see clients when you start your practice placement. If you are trying to fit this around full-time work, make sure you have the internal resources and the support of others to do so.

Counselling courses vary in their ethos and approach, so what you may have heard about one course (e.g. lots of experiential work) may not apply to others. If you find that your expectations are not being met then talk to the tutors about it – there may be something that can be done, something that you can do differently, or you may be able to adjust your expectations.

It is particularly important to acknowledge that counsellor training is not in itself therapy. There may be some therapeutic benefit for you as a side effect of aspects of your training, but training courses exist to train counsellors. (If you want therapy, see a therapist!) We are aware of some students whose motivation for undertaking training may have been less clear than one might hope – those who enter training primarily for their own therapy are rarely successful and may cause difficulties in the group.

For all that, it is reasonable to expect that, overall, counselling training will be an exciting, challenging and fulfilling experience, as a result of which you will learn a lot about yourself and about others, and will develop personal qualities and skills that will enable you to engage with clients and others at a deeper level. Training will prepare you for professional practice in a complex, rewarding and responsible role.

experience (as a factor in applying to a course)

▷ application forms, strengths

Courses vary in the kind of experience they look for, and in how explicit the tutors are (possibly how aware we are) about what kinds of experience count most. Some Diploma courses insist on certificate-level training as a prerequisite, for example; we think some students need to unlearn skills from earlier courses. More generally, it's not the experience itself that matters so much as what the applicant has taken from it and learned about himself or herself.

experiential groups

▷ groups, self-awareness, trust

Experiential groups are a significant element of many training courses. They are a way (but not the only way) to raise your awareness of the impact you have on others and that others have on you; to develop the qualities of empathy, acceptance and genuineness and to practise relating to others in ways which demonstrate these qualities; to get more in touch with your feelings; to practise skills related to empathy, challenge and negotiation; to explore some of your past experiences and present issues; to experience self-disclosure and the impact of others' responses to it; to learn from the experiences of others; to experience conflict and its resolution; and to learn about managing boundaries.

Clearly this is a long list of possible learning experiences, and for some the lack of clarity about what they might get out of a particular session can be confusing and frustrating. Others find it exciting. If experiential groups are part of your course, then you can gain the most from them not only by participating as fully as you feel able to, but also by retaining a part of your awareness for monitoring your responses as the experience unfolds. Try to stay in touch with what you are feeling, what choices you are making about what to say or do and what not to, how you edit what you say, and whether the experiences you have are familiar from other aspects of your life.

Experiential groups will vary in size, though 8 to 12 people is probably ideal. Group sessions commonly last between 1 and 2 hours on a regular basis, but may be longer if they are less frequent. They will have a facilitator, who may not be one of your regular tutors, but only involved with the experiential group. Facilitators have different styles. Some will take a fairly unstructured approach, allow a lot of space and enable the group to find its own direction. Others may prefer to use structured activities to facilitate interaction, sharing and exploration; then encourage the group to process the experience. A common approach is to use structured activities early in the life of the group and gradually move towards a less structured non-directive style.

Experiential groups will usually spend some time developing a contract or ground rules to operate by, covering issues such as confidentiality, relating to each other with respect and acceptance, participation in the group and its activities, and boundaries.

Some guidelines for participating in experiential groups are:

- Listen carefully to what others say.
- Stay in touch with your own feelings and responses.
- Try to show empathy and acceptance towards the others in the group and notice when this is difficult.
- Show acceptance towards yourself as well as others – notice when you have negative feelings and responses.
- Notice when you want to involve yourself in the group and when you want to avoid doing so.
- Challenge yourself to stretch – take risks that are challenging but not too challenging.
- Try to own what you say –
  - talk from 'I …' rather than making generalisations about the group ('We all feel …' etc.);

▷ own your feelings rather than attributing them to others (e.g. 'When you withdraw like that I feel frustrated' rather than 'You make me feel frustrated').

‣ Listen carefully to the language that you and others use, e.g. saying 'I can't' rather than 'I won't' or 'always' rather than 'often' etc.

‣ Be prepared to challenge others in a positive way, and to be challenged.

‣ Be alert to group processes such as scapegoating, splitting, projection, denial etc.

‣ Be prepared to give and receive constructive feedback.

‣ Reflect carefully on your experience and the group process – both within the group and afterwards.

e

f

failing an assessment item or a course

▷ **assertiveness, loss, rejection, strengths**

The reaction of one of our students to failing the final skills assessment was to want to burn down the building. This showed openness and sensitive self-awareness and illustrates how intense reactions to failure can be. She passed her resit well.

Any training programme that assesses against a set of standards must include provision for students who do not meet those standards. Professional training in particular needs to ensure that standards are clear and that they are applied, so that the public and other professionals can have confidence in the qualifications awarded, and so that those who pass can feel that they have gained something worthwhile, signifying a level of achievement and proficiency, from their training. It is almost inevitable, then, that some students will not meet those standards and will fail, either at the level of particular assessment items or the training programme overall.

The term 'failure' is of course loaded with meaning, and may be associated with shame or other stigma for many. To this end many training institutions use other terms such as 'refer' to identify a standard of performance on an assessment item which does not meet the pass criteria. The implication of 'refer' is that an opportunity or opportunities exist to redeem the situation and pass the assessment. Institutions vary in their regulations relating to referrals and the number of attempts allowed for reassessment, but in almost all cases it is possible to be referred on an item of assessment, pass it at a subsequent attempt, and successfully complete the course. If numerical marks or grades are applied to assessment results then it is likely that reassessment will be 'capped' at a basic 'pass' mark or grade. You should be given clear information about assessment regulations when you start a course, often in the course handbook, or accessible online, and it is wise to make sure that you understand these regulations as they apply to submission of assessments, reassessment opportunities, etc.

If you have been referred on a particular assessment item you can reasonably expect to receive some detailed and constructive feedback from the marker or another tutor which should enable you to understand clearly why you have not passed the assessment, and be aware of what you need to do, or do differently, in order to pass it.

Failing a course as a whole should therefore only occur when the opportunities to retake assessments which have been referred have been exhausted. We think that such 'failures' at the end of a training course should be relatively rare. It is good practice to design assessment schemes for training courses that assess students' progress and aptitude for the profession at a number of points along the way. The assessment scheme should enable students who do not have the qualities, skills, abilities, motivation or resilience to complete the programme to identify themselves or be identified as early as possible.

Clearly there is a balance to be struck here between allowing students to develop as individuals at different rates (and having sufficient flexibility in the assessment scheme to allow for this) on the one hand, and being fair to students by being realistic about their potential to successfully complete training (or not) on the other. For most students, 'failing' relatively early on a course and being unable to progress is likely to be less disappointing and stigmatising than investing time and effort in getting to the end of a course only to find that they are unable to pass the 'final hurdle'.

If you are concerned about your ability to complete a course we recommend that you discuss this as openly as you can with tutors, asking for realistic feedback, and consider it carefully. Assessments often require a variety of skills and qualities to pass, and it may be that specific help is available, for example in the area of academic/writing skills. Personal therapy may help with the personal development issues, and additional practice sessions may help with skills development; and often blocks can be overcome so that students who have struggled at some point on the course end up doing very well.

However, it is important to reflect on the effort required to keep going with a course if you are struggling, and consider whether it really is realistic and the best thing for you at this point in your life. Discussions with tutors, peers and close friends/family, or in personal therapy may help you to get perspective at such times.

fears about counsellor training

> ▷ assertiveness, beginning, client, distressed, expectations, relaxation,
> stress, trust, writing (expressive)

Counselling trainees may, especially at the beginning of a course, be afraid of, among other things, lacking skills, and being rejected, ridiculed, attacked, torn to pieces, incompetent and exposed. This is quite natural, as is people looking more confident and at ease than they feel. Talking or writing about a fear (or anxiety, or dread) will probably reduce or dispel it. Relaxation, by definition, certainly will, but there is a complex interaction between fear, trust, familiarity, the unknown, expressing the fear and being relaxed.

Simple relaxation techniques can be very effective, e.g. breathing more slowly and deeply, and 'attention out' (see the entry on Client, preparing for the training role of). Knowing that some of the others probably feel the same way and that physiologically your body is just getting ready for action (to fight or flee) may also help.

feedback, giving

▷ **language, skills versus qualities**

Giving feedback is an important skill to develop during counsellor training. Feedback can and does happen within a number of activities, but perhaps the most explicit and important use of peer feedback is in developing counselling skills. There are obvious benefits to peers from your giving clear and accurate feedback, but it also benefits you by developing your ability to observe counselling practice, reflect on and evaluate what you see, and communicate your sense of the strengths and areas for development clearly. These skills can then be applied to observation of your own practice. The ability to give appropriately sensitive feedback that achieves a balance between being supportive and being challenging can also benefit your relationships with clients.

Useful feedback needs to have the qualities shown in Table 2.

Table 2   *Important qualities for useful feedback*

Clear	Try to avoid being 'woolly' or overcomplicated – think about the message you want to communicate, and put it as simply as you can without unhelpful elaboration.
Specific	Useful feedback often identifies specific behaviours or instances and their impact, for example, 'When you said … I noticed …' This enables the recipient to consolidate strengths or consider concrete alternatives.
Owned	Communicate what you have to say as *your* feedback, not a statement of fact – this should help the recipient to weigh and evaluate the feedback without reacting defensively.
Constructive	Feedback should highlight 'areas for development' rather than 'weaknesses'. It is more useful for the recipient to hear what they might have done more/less/differently, than what they did wrong.
Balanced	Make sure you give feedback on what you thought was done well as well as what could be done differently – reinforcing strengths is more effective for developing skills than highlighting weaknesses.
Relevant	Feedback should be meaningful to the recipient, so try to establish what they are trying to practise/achieve. Focus on this and avoid the temptation to offer opinions on the client's issues etc.

The 'positive feedback sandwich' can be a useful structure for delivering feedback after a practice session in a way which can be heard and assimilated by the recipient. However, some people find it too structured and contrived. It is:

1 *Strengths*: what you thought was done well, with specific examples of skills/ impact etc.
2 *Areas for development*: what you thought might have been done better, again with specific examples and suggestions for alternatives.
3 *Summary of strengths*: end on a positive note so that the recipient is aware of what they have achieved and can continue to build on.

These guidelines can readily be transferred to the context of giving feedback within a therapeutic relationship, where there are established benefits for helping clients to acknowledge their strengths and resources (Egan 2010), or drawing clients' attention to positive change and encouraging them to take the view that this has happened as a result of something they have done (Hubble et al. 1999).

feedback, receiving and recording

▷ **assertiveness, self-awareness, stress**

Receiving feedback is a necessary part of any training course, but for trainee counsellors it has some particular features. Developing as a counsellor involves the acquisition of knowledge and skills in common with most professions, but the centrality of the therapeutic relationship in counselling means that trainees also need to receive feedback about aspects of their personal development, ways of being and relating to others. This can potentially seem threatening, and if delivered in an unskilled way, or received uncritically, it can leave you feeling vulnerable or deflated.

Sometimes even accurate and skilfully delivered feedback can sting – especially if it is at odds with your view of yourself or if it draws attention to areas you would prefer to avoid. It is important to develop a non-defensive way of responding. The most useful response in such cases is usually to make sure you have understood the feedback offered. You may wish to acknowledge the feelings you have in response, but should try to see the feedback as something potentially useful that has been offered to you, by reflecting separately on the content and on the impact it has had on you. We have both had experience of initially painful and difficult feedback leading to important new insights and opportunities for learning or personal development.

As a counsellor, it is vitally important to cultivate awareness of the impact that you are having on others (especially clients) and vice versa. Feedback and reflection are important ways of doing this, and you should aim to develop self-awareness and a self-concept which is able to integrate feedback from others without being vulnerable to sudden shifts as a result of each new piece of feedback. Structured opportunities for feedback will occur most obviously in skills practice sessions and tutorials, but may also be included in workshops and experiential sessions; and there are many informal opportunities for giving and receiving feedback. (Feedback from clients can of course be particularly valuable and review sessions should include opportunities to elicit this.)

Some general guidelines for receiving feedback are:

▸ Listen carefully to what is being said and ask for clarification, examples, details and specifics if you need to. ('Can you give me an example of when/ how I did that?')

▸ Try to listen in a balanced and non-defensive way. Make sure that you hear positives as well as criticisms, and listen for what is constructive when you are being offered criticism.

▸ Check that you have understood the feedback offered by paraphrasing or summarising.

▸ Try to avoid 'discounting' positive feedback ('Oh, it was nothing really, anyone could have ...' etc.) or defensively arguing with critical feedback. If feedback seems negative or unhelpful, try asking for it in a more constructive form, for example, 'How do you think I might have done that differently?'

▸ Once you have clearly understood the feedback offered, acknowledge it and show appropriate appreciation or thanks.

▸ Find an opportunity to reflect on and evaluate the feedback you have been given. It is your job to determine its relevance and usefulness – what you can learn from it, and how it can help in identifying future goals, plans etc.

It is likely that there will be a number of opportunities to record and process feedback during counsellor training, for example in a reflective journal, professional log, and records of supervision or skills practice sessions. You should try to record the feedback as accurately and as true to its original meaning as you can, before considering your response to it. Some students find the formula *What? – So what? – Now what?* a useful structure for processing feedback (as well as other experiences):

What?	Record the feedback given (or other experience) accurately.
So what?	Reflect on the feedback (or other experience). What might it mean to you? How does it relate to other feedback/experiences? How useful or relevant is it? How important is it? How much do you trust and value it? What questions does it raise?
Now what?	As a result of this reflection, what do you intend to do? This might include eliciting further feedback, setting goals and developing action plans, trying out new behaviours or focusing on the development of particular skills or qualities.

When keeping a journal or log, such processing can help you to develop a sense of continuity, intentionality and ownership of your learning/development, where feedback leads to reflection, goal setting, and action, which leads to further feedback etc. An example of this at a fairly straightforward level can be implemented in records of skills practice sessions, where the feedback from one session can be recorded and used in identifying goals for the next session, which can then be shared with the observer(s), leading to further specific and relevant feedback and so on. Below is an example of a skills lab log sheet, which can be used to record feedback and give some structure to the process of reflection.

LOG SHEET: SKILLS LABORATORY WORK

Date:

Activity/focus/goals for session:

Summary of feedback:

Personal reflection:

Aspects to develop: (learning goals)

1.

2.

3.

---

fees and funding

▷ **brochures, hours, intermitting, personal therapy**

It may be worth checking all the financial costs. Apart from the basic fee, these *may* include 'away days' or longer periods, personal counselling, extra supervision, travelling and books. Course brochures vary in how explicit they are about the fees and other costs.

Counsellor training costs students a few pounds an hour (e.g. say 200 hours per year for £2000). However, this can look rather less of a bargain when you're faced with the fee at the beginning of the course and paying for it yourself, if your income is reduced during the course or you've misjudged what you can afford. It may be worth asking for financial advice. Some students find that they can't afford to continue with their course, and have to intermit (see entry on Intermitting) or stop altogether.

Our experience is that nearly all counselling students pay their own fees. Occasionally, however, a student is persistent or lucky enough to find other sources of funding or partial funding. You could:

- ask the college about concessionary fees and bursaries;
- ask your employer (if you have one), obviously making out a case for the increased value to you or to your organisation of your studying counselling;

‣ find out about Career Development Loans or a related policy (contact the Department for Education and Employment (DfEE) or a participating bank);

‣ contact charities and trusts.

first day

▷ beginning of a course

frameworks

▷ integration, reading

A variety of conceptual frameworks are used by counsellors to assist in understanding client issues, formulating assessments and therapeutic plans, or keeping track of the therapeutic relationship and therapeutic process. Broadly speaking, these can be categorised as follows:

‣ Psychological theories, which attempt to explain some aspect or aspects of human behaviour, emotion, cognition, development, personality etc.

‣ Social/systems theories which address human interaction, behaviour in groups and the relationships between individuals and systems such as families, communities etc.

‣ Theories or frameworks of counselling/therapy which attempt to illuminate the dynamics of change or the process of therapy.

‣ Models or theories of health and well-being which may provide direction for therapeutic work in terms of goals or strategies, or focus on strengths and resources.

As a trainee counsellor or psychotherapist, you may find yourself confused by the vast array of conceptual frameworks available and referred to in the literature or by your tutors. This can be particularly problematic since the various frameworks used by counsellors do not always fit together comfortably. Indeed, there are many instances of conflicting assumptions between theoretical perspectives, and conflicting conclusions can be drawn about how to proceed in particular circumstances depending on which framework is applied.

You may therefore find yourself wishing for a 'grand theory of everything', which would point you in the right direction whatever the situation. Unfortunately, it appears that human beings and human society are too complex to be fully explained by any one theoretical framework (or at least not one that currently exists). Given that models/frameworks tend by their nature to reduce the complexity of that which is being modelled in order to represent it, this seems likely to continue to be the case.

Training courses tend to approach this issue in one of two ways. Some training courses will attempt to provide you with an in-depth understanding of a particular framework (or a limited set of frameworks which can be integrated with a reasonable degree of consistency), and with the skills, qualities or techniques used to implement that framework. Mention is likely to be made of other frameworks, but the emphasis is on developing knowledge and competence for a particular style of practice in some depth. (This may be a single counselling/therapy model such as person-centred therapy, or a particular 'theoretical integration' which attempts to form a coherent whole out of two or more selected frameworks.)

The alternative is to attempt to enable trainees to work with a range of conceptual frameworks, to select appropriate frameworks for use with particular clients, and to be able to move comfortably between them without experiencing conflict and confusion. In order to at least minimise conflict and confusion it seems to be helpful to provide some overarching structure for integration or 'meta-framework'. Examples of such a 'meta-framework' are integrative process models for counselling/psychotherapy (e.g. O'Brien and Houston 2000; Egan 2010); or the research-based 'Common Factors' paradigm (Hubble et al. 1999), which suggests developing a firm grounding in the skills and qualities needed for forming effective therapeutic relationships, and the ability to select and work with whatever conceptual frameworks and techniques are a good 'fit' with the client (i.e. which fit relatively comfortably with the client's expectations and pre-existing ways of understanding themselves, their lives, the world, the therapeutic process etc.).

freewriting

> journal, self-awareness, supervision

Freewriting is writing for several minutes whatever comes into your mind without stopping and without thinking about grammar and punctuation. If you're writing on a computer, Elbow (1997) suggests turning the screen down so that you can't see your words. The idea is to free yourself as much as you can from editing or evaluating – that can be done later, when the freewriting has given you something to work on. The result of freewriting is usually some useful bits – stimulating, well put – among lots of repetition and banality. That's fine: for most people, crossing out is crucial for good writing.

At one level, freewriting can help to 'keep your inner world awake'; at another, it can be a remedy for writer's block, or a way of preventing it. You may also like to suggest it as a creative or unblocking activity in a supervision group: everyone freewrites for, say, 5 minutes about their reaction to a particular client or problem, then selects (edits) the useful bits to discuss in the group (Murray 1997, 1998).

future of counselling

▷ choosing a career, counselling and coaching

If you are choosing to invest time, energy and money in training as a counsellor, it may be advisable to spend some time researching the current state and possible future of the profession. Counselling is probably better established, better accepted and more widely understood than it has been at any time in the past. Recent government initiatives have stressed the need for the provision of psychological support, including counselling services, in education and primary health care, and it is an established intervention in occupational health, addiction/dependence services and a range of other aspects of social care.

However, at the time of writing some uncertainties exist as to how things will develop in the next few years. Statutory regulation is very likely to be introduced shortly in the UK (currently planned for 2011) but at present it remains uncertain exactly what job titles will be regulated, and how a register will be structured (for example to what extent there will be distinctions between different types of therapists). It is clear, however, that the introduction of a register will have far-reaching consequences for the delivery of training courses, and for how counsellors describe themselves and promote or market their services. Being on the register will be of central importance to one's credibility and career prospects.

If you are entering training during the period when these developments are unfolding, you should look for information on the latest developments (for example via the BACP or HPC websites) and clarify the status of training courses you are considering. At present it seems highly likely that courses which are BACP accredited will in due course lead to admission to the register, but future procedures for HPC approval remain to be made clear.

The evidence-based practice (EBP) movement has provided impetus for counsellors to demonstrate the effectiveness of what they do, but in the future the profession would probably benefit from a widening of the perspective on what 'counts' as evidence and what questions are addressed. For example, the emergence of the 'common factors' from counselling research, and the importance of client and relationship factors in determining outcome, is rather at odds with the diagnosis–treatment paradigm which permeates much current thinking about EBP. See www.talkingcure.com for a wealth of information and discussion on this area.

Linked to EBP, cognitive behaviour therapy or CBT is seen in some quarters of the counselling community as a threat at present, and this perception has probably been reinforced by government initiatives to provide CBT widely through the NHS, on the basis of what is seen as positive evidence of its effectiveness. Therapists are being trained relatively quickly (compared to counsellor training) in order to deliver CBT, and in our experience more and more clients are now coming to therapy and asking specifically for CBT. A challenge to the counselling profession would seem to be the question of how best to respond to these developments.

Options include drawing attention to the research which indicates that other approaches are as effective as CBT in most cases; generating further research that meets the criteria for EBP; challenging the basis of EBP and campaigning for recognition of other paradigms; arguing for the importance of non-technique aspects of therapy (core skills, relationship etc.); and equipping ourselves with the knowledge, techniques and skills of CBT and integrating them into our practice.

Another identifiable trend, and one which we see as likely to continue, is the growth of one-to-one talking practices which share a great deal with counselling in terms of core skills, processes and theory/frameworks, but which can be identified as being distinctive in terms of their goals, boundaries and ethical frameworks, context, or target client group. Examples of these are coaching and mentoring. In some ways, such activities present opportunities to counsellors to broaden what they do, market their work in other areas, and possibly command higher fees. On the other hand, they may be seen as a threat in encroaching into areas where counselling is the appropriate intervention, and allowing individuals to practise without the rigour of counsellor training, supervision, boundaries and an ethical framework.

One development linked to the above is that the coaching movement in particular seems to have embraced the field of positive psychology very openly, and this is in turn beginning to be more evident as a development in counselling. Failure to do so could leave the counselling profession restricted to a reparative role – helping people to address problems – but without the important counterbalance of an emphasis on strengths, developing opportunities and maximising well-being, fulfilment etc. Egan (2010) has long been an advocate of a two-pronged approach: *The Skilled Helper* is subtitled 'A problem-management and opportunity-development approach to helping', and solution-focused therapy is explicit in its attention to the client's strengths, resources and achievements, seeking to build on what works rather than become preoccupied with what doesn't.

Counselling has been criticised in the past as being primarily a white, middle-class activity, and to some extent that criticism remains valid. However, there have been important developments in recent years both in the development of the provision of counselling for hard-to-reach groups such as some ethnic minorities, the socially deprived etc., and in the development of a body of literature addressing issues of difference and equality. In the future it is to be hoped that more counsellors emerge from the hard-to-reach groups and that the ethnic/social balance of the profession grows closer to that of the general population.

Dryden (1994) identified 14 possible future trends for counselling and counselling training, and it is both interesting and perhaps somewhat sobering to see how many of these remain relevant 15 years later (for example, developing a national register, increasing emphasis on evaluation, providing services for 'difficult to reach' groups, developing agreed standards for training, increasing emphasis on eclecticism and integration, and broadening the role and influence of counsellors through consultancy).

g
gender

▷ diversity, multiculturalism

The majority of students who enter counselling training in the UK are female. You may find yourself in a group where there are few (and occasionally even no) men. This can create some difficulties in that men may feel disadvantaged by being in a minority, and women may regret the relative lack of opportunities to practise with a male client in training groups. In spite of the views expressed by some that the counsellor qualities of empathy, acceptance and genuineness might be seen as more feminine than masculine, there is no convincing evidence to suggest that therapy outcomes are related to the gender of the therapist. There is some evidence that male and female counsellors may tend to show some differences in their approach and preference for using certain specific skills or interventions, but this does not appear to influence their likely success.

Of more importance is to note that some clients may have a preference for a counsellor of a particular gender, for example women with a history of abuse by males may prefer a female counsellor, and clients who wish to work on issues of a sexual nature may prefer to work with a counsellor of the same gender (or they may not). Clients have a right to express their preferences about the counsellor they work with and you should try to avoid feeling rejected or inadequate if it turns out that some clients do not wish to work with you because of your gender.

Feminist approaches to counselling have developed as a result of the view that many of the issues a woman may bring to counselling are a direct or indirect result of inequality and patriarchy in society. Feminist approaches vary, but mainly originate from a humanistic tradition and are intended to enable women to make their own choices, fulfil their potential, and to explore and address issues related to gender roles, discrimination or inequality. See Bruna Seu (2006) for an overview.

good counsellors

▷ assertiveness, choosing a counselling orientation, motives, selection, strengths

For trainee counsellors, or prospective trainees, the main implications of ideas and research on good counsellors are:

1 There are lots of ways of being a good counsellor.
2 Considerable practice is needed to be a great counsellor – according to Miller et al. (2008) this means 10,000 hours or approximately 10 years.
3 However, good (i.e. competent rather than great) counsellors are also needed.
4 Natural talent and natural desire to practise so much may be interrelated.

One way of interpreting the idea of a 'good counsellor' is as someone with a special set of qualities. You may like to pause and consider your view of what these qualities might be.

There have been a few studies of master therapists, as nominated by other counsellors (the method used by Jennings and Skovholt 1999) or chosen for their effectiveness with clients (e.g. Miller et al. 2008). Miller et al. argued, following the work of Ericsson on athletes, pianists and many other occupational groups, that what they called 'supershrinks' are *not* the particularly gifted or talented, but those who practise much more and in a more focused way. In particular, supershrinks set themselves objectives which are appropriately challenging, and they get clear feedback on the results. They follow up their work and check their actual rates of success. So the 'formula for success' that they propose (Miller et al. 2008: 7) is:

> 1 Determine your baseline of success.
> 2 Engage in deliberate practice.
> 3 Get feedback.

Assuming for the moment that their argument is sound, this looks easier for trainee counsellors to put into practice than it does for counsellors: trainees are routinely asked to reflect systematically on their work and it is assessed and commented on. However, Miller et al. see it as quite straightforward for practitioners too, 'using simple paper and pencil scales and some basic statistics' (p. 7).

They then make two particularly encouraging points. First, that several studies suggest that 'most clinicians do good work most of the time'; and second, that regularly monitoring client progress improves effectiveness dramatically.

The next point in their argument comes close to a central issue in how skill develops: are there relatively stable qualities that differentiate between good counsellors and average or relatively poor counsellors, or is it, as Ericsson says, a matter of lots of practice with good (i.e. accurate and systematic) feedback? Miller et al. say that 'Supershrinks … are exquisitely attuned to the vicissitudes of client engagement. In what amounts to a quantum difference between themselves and average therapists, they are much likelier to ask for and receive negative feedback about the quality of the work and their contribution to the alliance' (p. 8).

We like the emphasis on open discussion of the counsellor–client relationship, especially when it's 'going wrong' (and the underlying collaborative tone that is implied) but we also think it raises the questions of whether such 'exquisite attunement' (sensitivity, non-defensiveness) is going to result from practice alone, and whether personal qualities really are an irrelevant or minor factor.

A further and related question, which is also a strong criticism in our view of Ericsson's and Miller et al.'s argument, is: 'Where does the motivation come from to put in the much greater number of hours of practice?' Miller et al. (2008) go some way towards recognising this criticism: 'What leads people to devote the time, energy and resources to achieve greatness is poorly understood' (p. 9). Here, we think that the notions of 'talents' and 'strengths' are valuable while also recognising the value of the idea (and research) about practising a lot, seeking feedback, reflecting on the feedback to come up with strategies that might be more effective, and acting on them.

Taking the 'talent' approach a little further, psychological type theory implies that there are many different ways of being a 'good counsellor': that counsellors of each type tend to have characteristic strengths and corresponding weaknesses (Bayne 2004). For example, empathy is said to be more natural and comfortable for some types and challenging for other (opposite) types – when both empathy and challenge are valuable in counselling as it is generally defined.

The more pluralistic approach of psychological type theory is compatible with some general qualities and also with an approach emphasising feedback and collaboration (but not the rejection of talent and individual differences sometimes associated with it). Overall, though, the essential personal qualities of good counsellors are unclear so far (Lambert and Ogles 2004; McLeod 2009) and they may be very complicated, e.g. varying with different counselling orientations, client problems, client personalities and different stages of counselling.

groups

▷ experiential groups, self-awareness, trust

h

hidden agendas

▷ **assertiveness, feedback, motives, self-awareness, trust, values**

Hidden agendas are goals which are not expressed or owned. An individual may be trying to achieve something but not wish others to be aware of it, or indeed may not be fully aware of it themselves. In counselling training and counselling in general, hidden agendas can be seen as problematic as they are not associated (by definition) with genuineness and openness, but can lead to indirect or manipulative behaviour on one side, and confusion, frustration or resentment for other people. Skilful feedback, encouraging others to be explicit about their goals, and practising this for yourself should help.

As a counsellor, you should of course not have hidden agendas for your clients, although this can be a temptation if you feel that you know what is best for them, or have a sense that they are making a mistake in some decision. Usually, there are ways to deal with such feelings, provided that this can be done without exerting influence over the client. For example: 'I hope you don't mind me saying this, but I'm aware I have some uneasiness about what you are planning. I wonder how it is for you?'

If you are aware of regularly and powerfully having goals on behalf of your clients (beyond the generic goals of increasing happiness, fulfilment, choice, autonomy etc.) you may need to explore this in supervision, reflect on your motivation for training as a counsellor, and explore whether you can really believe in and act on the core value of client self-determination. We have observed a number of students early in their training who seem to feel that having hidden agendas for clients is a good thing, offering feedback in skills training along the lines of, 'I like the way you managed to get him to talk about ...' or 'You managed to keep the focus on ... even though she was trying to avoid it.' With experience you should aim to become more confident in sharing responsibility with clients in sessions, deciding together what to talk about, drawing attention to perceived resistance and working together on whether and how to address it.

hours of study

▷ **reading, time management**

A question we sometimes ask in selection interviews is 'If we offer you a place, what will you do less of?' The implication (which is realistic) is that counsellor training is demanding of time as well as intellectually and emotionally. As well as your time at the course itself, perhaps 6 hours a week, there is private study and coursework, client hours of probably 2 or 3 hours a week plus supervision at the agency, travelling to and from the course etc., and for some students and some courses, personal counselling.

h

i

imagery and inability to visualise

▷ disability, exercises

Imagery, also called visualisation, is used in many approaches to counselling and sometimes in training and supervision. One of us remembers vividly his inability, in a counselling conference workshop, to visualise, and the presenter's scornful and dismissive reaction, 'You'll be able to if you practise.' I resented it at the time, but now I think she just didn't know that some people visualise well (distinctly, almost as though watching TV), others more fuzzily, and some not at all.

An inability to visualise may, for some people, be a matter of practice, but for others it is a (relatively mild) disability and can be an upsetting discovery. If you are one of this group and your tutor uses imagery and doesn't know about this individual difference, you can tell them. What non-imagers do instead is 'feel' (mentally) people, objects and scenes, which means that we can take part in imagery exercises to some extent.

It seems, informally, from asking each year of our course, to be about one person in 20 who doesn't visualise. If you want to try improving your ability to visualise, try a simple image first, e.g. look at an object, study it closely, then close your eyes and try to 'hold it'. We don't know of any research on how effective this approach is or on correlates of different levels of imaging skill. For discussions of imagery, see Payne (2000) and Hall et al. (2006).

integration

▷ developing your own model

The term 'integration' is used in counselling and psychotherapy to describe the use of concepts, theories and explanatory frameworks from a *range* of approaches or schools of thought. Integration is generally used to describe the application of some overarching 'integrating framework' that enables ideas to be brought together in an organised and systematic way, and is sometimes contrasted with 'eclectic', which would indicate a more open (and less systematic) approach to borrowing techniques and processes from a wide range of sources.

Horton (2006b) describes two rather different approaches to integration. 'Theoretical integration' refers to the bringing together of two or more specific theoretical approaches or frameworks to create a new integrated framework, whereas 'open-system integration' provides an organising system (often in the form of a model describing the *process* of therapy) within which a wide range of techniques and conceptual frameworks can be applied. So, for example, if you are undertaking integrative training, your course may be based on an 'in-house' integrative model which has been developed by the tutors to bring together ideas from person-centred therapy about the core therapeutic relationship with concepts from psychodynamic therapy which are intended to illuminate the origins of client issues. This is an example of theoretical integration.

On the other hand, a model such as Egan's Skilled Helper Model is intended as the basis for open-systems integration. Once you have learned to use the Skilled Helper Model, the intention is that it is possible to integrate 'whatever is ethical and works' in terms of techniques and explanatory frameworks from other approaches.

There is some potential for confusion around the use of the terms 'integrative' and 'eclectic' and authors use them in different ways or even on occasions interchangeably. This is unfortunate, but you might wish to clarify the precise way the terms are used on your course, and bear in mind that some of the sources you read could well be using the terms differently.

integrative counselling

> ▷ choosing a counselling orientation, core model, criticisms of counselling,
> developing your own model

Research into the effectiveness of counselling and psychotherapy shows that generally the main approaches are equally effective (Lambert 2004; Cooper 2008). It seems that 'common factors', and the extent to which these are practised by individual therapists (among whom there is wide variation in effectiveness), explain how counselling works.

Hubble et al. (1999) make the case that where approach and technique do influence the outcome of therapy, this tends to be mainly on the basis of how well the chosen approach fits with the client's worldview, how they understand their problems, and how they see the process of change. Approaches or techniques that are a good fit with the client's 'personal psychological model' are more likely to be successful.

This seems to be a strong argument for integrative counselling, in that it is reasonable to expect that integrative practitioners will have a wider range of frameworks and techniques at their disposal which they can offer to clients, and thus a better chance of securing such a 'good fit'. It also reinforces the desirability of working with techniques on the basis of 'informed consent', recognising the client's right to take part in decisions about how they are to be helped: to set their own goals, to understand the techniques which might be used to help them, and to exercise choice about which techniques are used (Jinks 2006).

The 'common factors' research suggests that while client variables and events outside of therapy are the strongest predictors of outcome, the quality of the therapeutic relationship, particularly as perceived by the client, is the most important factor over which the counsellor can have some direct influence (Lambert 2004). This suggests that the qualities and skills for developing and using the relationship should be the foundation of integrative counselling (and indeed all approaches).

Another factor category which is quite strongly linked to counselling outcome is what Hubble et al. (1999) refer to as expectancy and placebo effects – i.e. the hope engendered by engaging in counselling, and being offered a convincing framework suggesting that things can get better. Counsellors can try to mobilise this effect by treating clients as capable and resourceful and encouraging them to see themselves in such a way; building motivation and a sense of hope by helping them to develop a vision of a better future; drawing attention to positive change as it occurs and encouraging clients to see it as a result of something they have done; and conveying appropriate confidence in the approaches and techniques they offer.

intermitting

> ▷ choosing a career, decisions, loss

'Intermitting' is a term used in many institutions for taking some time out from a course or programme. This is generally at the discretion of the programme leader, although there may be other procedures involved, and would be offered in response to changes in personal or health circumstance which make it difficult to continue with the course at the present time (but which are likely to be temporary).

The principle of intermission is that when circumstances have improved, you can return to the course at or near the point where you left it, pick things up and continue. There is generally a time limit on how long the break can be – a 2-year maximum is common – and there may be specified points at which you can return, for example the beginning of a semester or module. If you are struggling with your course for personal or health reasons, and there is a likelihood that things will improve in the medium if not the short term, then you may benefit from intermission.

Some potential disadvantages are that you will be rejoining a different and probably established group, you will be likely to lose the support of your current peers, will experience a discontinuity in your training, may have to get to know different tutors, and may indeed find it difficult to follow through with the decision to return when the time comes. The first steps are to discuss options with your tutor, find out what the policy on intermission is at your training institution, and explore other ways you might cope and get support through your current difficulties.

interpersonal process recall (IPR)

> ▷ assertiveness, feedback, role play, video/DVD

IPR involves playing back a video or audio tape recording of a counselling session, usually (on a course) a practice session between two students, and remembering, with help, what was going on 'beneath the surface'. Barker (1985) encapsulated the underlying assumption when he stated that 'accompanying even apparently trivial dialogue there seems to be an enormous breadth and depth of thoughts, feeling and fantasies – often of a surprisingly primitive nature – that are often quickly forgotten or suppressed' (p. 155). Increased awareness of these feelings etc. is potentially of great value for developing counselling qualities and skills.

IPR was developed by Kagan. He described how, when his university was one of the few with professional video recording equipment, lectures by eminent speakers were recorded to preserve them for future use. The speakers were often curious and asked to see and hear themselves in action. They were amazed at the detail and extent to which the recordings were able to stimulate their recall of the experience and frequently remarked on discrepancies between how they remembered feeling at the time and what they actually said and did at a particular moment. Kagan (1984) explained that as they were eminent speakers he felt able only to make respectful inquiries and encourage them to elaborate rather than offer any feedback or evaluation as he might have done with students. This way of 'inquiring' became a crucial feature of IPR.

There are two main roles in the basic form of IPR: Recaller and Inquirer.

The Recaller role

A central feature of IPR is that the control over when and where to stop the tape, and over how far the exploration should go, lies entirely with the Recaller. In this way you review your own tape as much or as little as you wish, and are responsible for your own self-discovery and learning.

The Inquirer role

The process of recall is facilitated by a neutral third party, someone who was not involved in the original interaction. This person is known as the Inquirer. While listening to the playback, the Inquirer waits until the person reviewing decides to stop the tape and then, by using a series of probing but non-interpretative, neutral questions, invites them to recall, clarify and explore their experience.

The Inquirer role is easier to conceptualise than to actually perform. It consists entirely of asking brief, open-ended exploratory questions: no empathy or challenging. IPR assumes that Recallers are the best authority on their own inner self-awareness and will choose to respond to or reject any of the questions offered. It also recognises that the Recaller may not be able, or might not want, to take up some of the questions. That is fine. The task is to facilitate the Recaller's own self-discovery and not to be drawn into counselling, 'active listening', giving information or even sharing observations. It can also be treated as practice in developing intuition.

Recallers are helped to explore three dimensions of the interaction recorded on tape: what was going on within themselves, what was going on within the other person, and what was going on between them. The focus is on the Recaller's reaction 'then', at the point at which the tape was stopped, rather than 'now', within the recall session. The questions seek to help the participant recall thoughts and feelings rather than specific behaviours.

Inquirer leads

Some of the indicative questions from Kagan's checklist of 'often-used Inquirer leads' include:

> What were you thinking at that moment?
> What were you feeling?
> What pictures or memories went through your mind?
> What did you think the other person was feeling?
> What did you want the other person to think or feel?
> Was there anything you wanted to say but couldn't find appropriate words for?
> Did you have any physical sensations then?
> Where in your body did you most feel the impact?
> What had you hoped would happen next?
> Had you any goals or intentions at this point?

Other leads invite the Recaller to take their initial response more deeply, exploring mutual perceptions and whether there was any special meaning or possible associations:

> What prevented you from saying what you really wanted to say?
> What effect did that perception have on you?
> How do you think the other person was feeling/thinking about you?
> Do you think he or she was aware of your feelings?
> What do you think she or he wanted you to think, feel or do?
> Do you think your description of the interaction would be the same as the other person's?
> Does that feeling have any special meaning for you? Is it familiar?
> Does she/he remind you of anyone else in your life?

Further practical points

The client can stay for the IPR session but usually, especially in early work with IPR, leaves the room. Preparation for IPR can usefully include some recognition and discussion of what this might be like and what the client might do while they wait to rejoin their group.

It is probably desirable for the Recaller to make a note of any ideas and insights. Here there is a balance between interrupting the flow of the inquiring and remembering the 'good bits'.

Variations of IPR

One variation is for clients to be Recallers too. This recall session is recorded and then used by the counsellor to learn about the client's perceptions and experience of the counsellor's behaviour and interventions. Alternatively, the Inquirer could report back to the counsellor.

A further variation is mutual recall, in which both the counsellor and the client participate in the same recall session with an Inquirer. They are both asked to share their recalled thoughts and feelings, paying attention to how they perceived each other and what meanings they attribute to each other's behaviour. This is the most advanced form of IPR; it requires self-awareness, empathy, sensitivity to the other person and the courage or assertiveness to share experiences and reactions to the other person. In counsellor and client recall, participants develop the ability to talk openly and non-defensively about the relationship between counsellor and client. Counsellors learn about their interpersonal impact, how they come across to others; and learn to talk directly and explicitly about the relationship itself.

j

journal
▷ assessment, assertiveness, self-awareness, stress, time management, writing (expressive)

Various forms of journal or diary are used in counsellor training (Daniels and Feltham 2004). Rainer (1978) saw a journal as 'a practical psychological tool that enables you to express feelings without inhibition, recognize and alter self-defeating habits of mind, and come to know and accept that self which is you' (p. 18). There are many ways of writing a journal, including 'games you can play with your inner consciousness to get to know it better' (Rainer 1978: 26). Some examples from Rainer (1978), Adams (1990) and Waines (2004) are:

1 Lists, e.g. of desires, things you feel uneasy about, things you're happy about, beliefs you've discarded, loves.
2 'Portraits', e.g. describe a friend.
3 Describe a day.
4 At the end of a day, write one adjective to describe it and another to describe how you'd like the next day to be.
5 Freewriting: write quickly and without stopping or editing.
6 Sit quietly for a few moments before writing (to allow the most important incidents and feelings to begin to surface).
7 Write with your other hand (the idea – not yet tested rigorously as far as we know – is to improve contact with emotions).
8 Write about yourself in the third person.
9 Write dialogue, e.g. with someone else or between part of you and another part of you.

Like all self-awareness techniques, writing a journal is much more enjoyable and effective for some people than others. It is sometimes experienced as oppressive. There may be room for negotiation about format with the tutor responsible for the journal on your course.

Problems with writing your journal

Some people love journal writing; others find it at best a chore. Privacy, frequency and time are some of the problems sometimes experienced with the journal.

Privacy is a concern partly that partners or family members (who probably also feature in the journal) will read it, and partly that the tutor and external examiner will. Like all problems, worries about privacy can be written about in the journal! Underlying concerns usually then emerge, for example fear of embarrassment, regret about less spontaneity, more censorship, fear of others being hurt or angry by your honesty, or all of these and more.

One student's solution (or at least strategy) was to write on the first page 'THIS IS <u>PRIVATE</u>. READ IT AT YOUR PERIL'; another's was to buy a lockable diary; and another's to discuss their dilemma with their partner and reach an agreement. Obviously, questions of trust and openness are central.

Frequency is usually an easier problem. It's a matter of experimenting. For some people a set time, daily or weekly, works; for others, mood is the key factor. Time is, of course, a more general problem, discussed in the entry 'Time management'.

The general strategy that we recommend for problems with writing a journal, and generally, is to apply an integrative model of counselling in three stages:

> *Stage 1*: Write freely (explore and clarify, especially emotions) about the 'problem'.
>
> *Stage 2*: Analyse and perhaps challenge what you've written in stage 1, e.g. ask questions like:
>
> ‣ What other ways are there of looking at what happened?
> ‣ What is the evidence for and against any assertions?
> ‣ Any familiar feelings or patterns?
> ‣ Any relevant important values?
>
> *Stage 3*: Possible actions. Generate possible actions, which may be strategies to resolve or manage the problem, or to explore it further. Make the actions specific (e.g. how, when, who) and consider *doing* one or two of them.

That's the basic structure (Bayne et al. 2008 give a worked example in the section on expressive writing). Additional, valuable skills are to write summaries and to follow up and evaluate actions.

I

language and linguistics

▷ interpersonal process recall, non-verbal communication, skills

Counselling is usually (though not exclusively) based on verbal communication, and learning to pay careful attention to the use of language, both your own and your client's, is an important aspect of training. The techniques of Conversation Analysis (see for example Ten Have 2007) can reveal valuable insights for counsellors by examining what is being said and how it is being said, in some detail.

Awareness of some of the principles and results of conversation analysis can help you to fine tune your listening skills and enable you to hear more of the whole message which the client is communicating. This includes the choices they are making about particular ways of constructing a sentence, particular choices of words which may indicate underlying intentions or assumptions, and the intonations, inflections, pauses and so on which add colour and emphasis to what is being said. A simple example is the way in which ending a sentence with a rising tone tends to indicate that it is in some way being offered as a question, and so may be a sign that the client is interested and willing to explore that particular point further.

Such attention to detail can also help you in maintaining an effective dialogue with clients, including picking out appropriate points to 'take a turn' to speak without interrupting or talking over the client, and structuring your own interventions in ways which complement that of the client. Again at a simple level, an example is that a client who speaks in a low tone with frequent pauses may be discouraged or overwhelmed by responses that are by contrast fast and animated. Such adjustments are for most people to some extent instinctive, but for counsellors, who need to be particularly skilled at developing rapport through communication, an understanding and awareness of the processes operating can be invaluable.

The relationship between thinking and speech is complex, but it is to some extent two-way, in that what one says does have an impact on what one thinks. So, for example, if a client says 'Nothing I do ever goes right', it is probably not an indication of a firmly held belief and, if challenged, they would probably acknowledge that at least sometimes, some of the things they do, do go right. But if it is not challenged, it is likely that the client's thoughts will proceed as if it were true, and the conversation will continue based on the assumption that nothing the client ever does goes right.

Such challenges may not be a problem if the aim of the dialogue is for the client to get in touch with and express their negative feelings, but if it is rather to explore possibilities for the future and to think about ways forward, it could be a significant handicap. At times like this some counsellors might therefore encourage the client to try saying something like 'I feel frustrated because often the things I try to do don't work out' and then talk about what it feels like to phrase it in that way. A similar approach can be taken with statements like 'I can't...' (try 'won't ...' or 'don't want to ...') or 'I'll have to ...' (try 'I'll choose to ...') etc.

This change of perspective can be particularly important in relation to ownership of feelings. The statement 'My boss makes me scared' communicates the client's feelings in relation to her boss, but it does so in a way that implies that the boss is responsible for the feelings, and the client is powerless in the situation. An alternative such as 'When my boss is angry, I feel scared' is different in two significant ways. First, it specifies the circumstances in which the fear is present more clearly – so it is not simply the presence of the boss, but it is particularly when the boss is angry, and by implication perhaps not at other times. Secondly, it locates responsibility for the feeling with the client. Being scared is the client's response to the boss being angry, not an inevitable consequence; and the client could potentially work on developing a different response. From a therapeutic point of view, the second version opens up a lot more options for progress than the first.

We are not suggesting here that you insist that clients express themselves in particular ways, but that there may be benefits to tentatively encouraging them to experiment with different ways and reflect on their underlying or embedded assumptions. Also, we hope you will see that this discussion offers a strong argument for (almost) never using the question 'And how does that make you feel?'

In terms of your own communication, the difference between asking closed and open questions is a simple example of how careful choice of structure can be important. Socially, closed questions are more common than open ones, and people frequently respond to closed questions with a more extended answer (rather than the 'yes' or 'no' that is invited). However, in counselling, the choice can be crucial in determining how a conversation unfolds. Consider the difference between asking a client 'Can you think of a way to make your boss less scary?' and 'What ways can you think of to feel more confident when your boss is angry?' It would be relatively easy for a client to respond negatively to the first question ('Not really, no, I can't'); but the second, with its open question structure, emphasis on a positive feeling (rather than the absence of a negative one), location of the change with the client rather than the boss, and specificity about the circumstances, is much more likely to elicit a positive and helpful response.

These examples are a simple starting point and the exploration of language and conversation can develop your listening and counselling skills in many ways. As a starting point, try listening out for embedded assumptions, presuppositions and generalisations in everyday conversation. Listen to skilled interviewers and reflect on the way in which their phrasing of a question is designed to elicit a particular sort of answer. When examining recordings or transcripts of your counselling practice, think carefully about the way the client is constructing what they say and how it might relate to their thinking and feeling; reflect on how your interventions might be leading the client towards a particular type of response, and consider the impact that alternatives might have had.

lifeline exercise

▷ **exercises, self-awareness, trust**

This exercise is intended to encourage you to reflect on formative experiences, people, events, changes, transitions etc. that have shaped your life. It is a useful exercise for training groups early in a course, both for raising self-awareness and to promote sharing and trust within the group. It can also be adapted for use with clients in counselling, where it encourages the client to reflect on their path to where they are now, and enables the counsellor to get to know something of the client's sense of their life narrative.

Plenty of space is desirable, e.g. two sheets of flipchart joined at the shorter side.

Instructions

Individually:

1 Draw a horizontal line across the middle of your paper, and divide into a scale for your age in 5- or 10-year intervals, starting at your birth and ending today.

2 Take some time to reflect on different phases of your life and identify the key events or influences that you can recall. Consider which you are comfortable to share with others in the group.

3 Place these on the lifeline – you may like to locate broadly positive experiences above the line, and more difficult ones below.

4 Give each identified event a name and either write short notes about what you recall or draw a picture/image/symbol to represent it.

5 Reflect on what you now see as the most important events. What were the antecedents and consequences? What feelings were around for you?

In small groups or pairs:

1 Take turns to talk through the events on your lifeline, describing as much as you feel comfortable with about what happened, how it felt, what led up to it, what followed, how you feel it has influenced you.

2 Other members of the group can ask questions to clarify their understanding, and comment on their responses to what is being described. Try to avoid the temptation to analyse and interpret.

Reflections on the exercise

▸ What did it feel like to do this exercise? What seemed positive and what was difficult about it?

▸ What have you learned or what new insights have you gained as a result?

▸ Are you aware of any patterns or themes to your life/experience/response to events etc. as a result?

▸ Can you identify any areas you would like to focus on now or in the future as targets for change or development? Can you identify any specific goals?

loss

▷ decisions, failing, rejection, relationships

Loss can take many forms – for example loss of youth, of children leaving home, of a job or status, of faith, of lifestyle, friendship, or property – and many issues brought to counselling include a theme of loss. Loss can also be an issue for students in counsellor training. You may experience an identifiable loss such as those listed above, or a bereavement, but you may also experience less obvious losses associated with transition to a new phase of your life, changes to your self-concept, new insights, or changes to significant relationships. You may also become aware of how a past loss is continuing to affect you and decide to work on it.

Bereavement is a particular form of loss, but many of the principles that apply to bereavement can also be applied to more general cases of loss. The work of Worden (2008) on grief and mourning identifies four 'tasks' of mourning, which can readily be adapted to loss in general. Worden's approach has some advantages in approaching how to cope with loss in that his tasks specify what needs to be *done* in order to make an effective transition, rather than identifying 'stages' which one passes through (a conceptual framework which can seem more passive and something to be *experienced*).

Worden's (2008) tasks of mourning can be framed for loss in general as follows:

1 *Accept the reality of the loss*, working through any denial or minimisation which may occur.
2 *Experience the feelings associated with the loss.* These can include sadness, anger, guilt, betrayal, anxiety, confusion and many other emotions, or complex combinations.
3 *Adjust to the new environment in which the loss has occurred.* This will include changes to patterns of thinking and behaviour, taking into account the practical impact of what is now lost.
4 *Psychologically 're-locate' the loss and move on with life.* This does not necessarily imply 'getting over' the loss (for example ending your relationship with a deceased loved one) but is about finding an appropriate place in your emotional life for what has been lost, enabling you to go on living effectively.

The tasks are quite complex and likely to overlap. Often they are revisited at successively deeper levels while working through a loss. So, for example, after the break-up of a romantic relationship, you might have accepted the break-up, but still be struggling with accepting that it is over for good, and be experiencing anger, regret and guilt, but not yet facing the sadness that is to come.

You might also be aware of a need to sort out financial and living arrangements in the short term, but later have to deal with the readjustment of mutual friendships, and searching for meaning in the experience and learning that can be carried forward to future relationships, and ultimately develop an internal model of the lost partner that can be carried forward perhaps with love and affection, but without prejudicing future relationships.

We see the 'tasks of mourning' model as useful in keeping track of the complexity of loss and enabling one to feel more empowered as one works through the process. Reviewing the tasks can sometimes help to identify what has not been completed successfully and therefore why a particular loss is continuing to affect a person's ability to live fully. It should of course be noted that not everyone experiences intense anxiety, depression or grief after a serious loss, and many continue to be psychologically well adjusted (Wortman and Silver 1989). Wortman and Silver identify several myths about coping with loss (for example that distress and working through are necessary, and that recovery or resolution are inevitable) and stress the great variability of individual reactions.

Many factors influence an individual's experience of and ability to cope with loss, including:

- *demographic and personal factors* such as age, gender, ethnic background, socioeconomic status, ego strength, emotional maturity, religious affiliation and previous experience of loss and coping;
- *social and contextual factors*: the presence or absence of support networks and the availability of help;
- *characteristics of the event*: predictability, intensity, how suddenly it happened, the extent to which it can be influenced or controlled.

Positive transitions can also involve an element of loss, as even desired changes often involve letting go of some things which are valued. Sugarman (2001) describes a general model for life transitions, suggesting that there is a generally recognisable sequence of responses accompanying a wide range of transitions, which includes elements of loss. The initial phases are concerned with attachment to the past, before a 'letting go' phase, which is followed by gradual adaptation to the new situation. There are many other similar models relating to specific situations.

m

membership organisations

The two main professional bodies for counsellors in the UK are the British Association for Counselling and Psychotherapy (BACP) and the UK Council for Psychotherapy (UKCP), and your course may be associated with one of them. We think it is worth checking their websites and considering becoming a student member. The potential benefits include newsletters and journals, e.g. BACP's *Therapy Today* and *Counselling and Psychotherapy Research Journal*, and the less tangible sense of belonging to an organisation that represents and influences a profession that matters to you.

mental health and mental health problems

▷ **diversity, stress**

As a counsellor you will inevitably be concerned with the mental health and well-being of your clients. In the main this will involve helping them to work towards improvements in well-being and the alleviation of whatever problem or issues they wish to work on. However, it is likely that you will also encounter some clients who are experiencing specific mental health problems. These may be the subject of an existing psychiatric diagnosis, or it may be that you become aware of aspects of a client's thinking, feeling or behaviour which seem to indicate a mental health problem.

When this is the case, you need to think carefully about the appropriateness of counselling as a therapeutic intervention. Daines et al. (2007) argue that a psychiatric diagnosis per se should not be seen as a contraindication for counselling, but that what needs to be considered is the nature and scope of the work to be undertaken and the extent to which the client can engage with the processes of counselling and derive some benefit. It may be that, in an extreme case, a client whose experience of reality is greatly at odds with that of the counsellor (perhaps due to hallucinations and delusional ideas), and who has little or no insight into their situation, may present an impossible challenge even to an experienced counsellor. In such cases counselling has the potential to do more harm than good, perhaps by raising levels of conflict or distress for the client, or inadvertently reinforcing delusions.

However, when some level of insight is present, as it generally is, counselling can provide meaningful help to clients experiencing mental health problems.

This can be at the level of addressing issues in day-to-day living, developing coping strategies for managing symptoms, or working with clients' emotions.

A key issue for a trainee counsellor is coming to terms with the range of perspectives on mental health issues, and the sometimes heated debate on how best to conceptualise mental health problems (or mental disorders, mental illnesses). In essence, this often boils down to a debate between the Western medical model, with its established procedures of assessment of symptoms → diagnosis → treatment → prognosis, and other perspectives, which might be described as social, or holistic, models. We think it useful to note that if we are genuinely to work from the client's frame of reference, it is helpful not to be too fixed into one way of looking at these issues, but rather be open to working in ways which are supportive of the client's own worldview. We have encountered some clients who have felt stigmatised and whose self-esteem has been adversely affected by a psychiatric diagnosis; and others who were greatly relieved to find that there was a name for what they had been experiencing, and that they were not alone in their symptoms.

Mental health problems can present a challenge to working in a person-centred way, in that it may become apparent that the client's worldview is in some ways the source of some of their difficulties. For example, imagine a client who, during depressed episodes, sees herself as worthless and nothing but a burden to her friends and family. Clearly, it is unlikely to be helpful if her counsellor only responds empathically to this experience and then works with her as though this were an accurate perception. From a person-centred viewpoint, this is a situation where the counsellor needs to strike a careful balance between the core conditions of empathy, unconditional positive regard, and congruence. Empathy would enable the counsellor to be in touch with the client's feelings and to respond in ways which demonstrate understanding of those feelings, but it can be important in such cases to separate understanding of feelings from unquestioning acceptance of the worldview that appears to go with the feelings.

Mental health problems will sometimes lead counsellors into a situation where they are in contact with other professionals, for example if the client becomes suicidal or otherwise presents a risk to themselves or someone else (see BACP Ethical Framework). In such situations we suggest that it is helpful for the counsellor to be familiar with the language and concepts of the medical model in order to be able to communicate effectively and have credibility. A number of useful books exist (e.g. Daines et al. 2007) which will help you to familiarise yourself with this language, the various perspectives on mental health and mental illness, and the signs and symptoms of various disorders.

Probably the most important thing for a trainee counsellor is to be able to recognise the signs of a serious mental health problem. Whilst it is not the counsellor's job to diagnose, it is important to be able to recognise when altered mood or perceptions, obsessive thoughts, hallucinatory experiences or delusional thinking are present to a degree that could disrupt the counselling process. Your supervisor will be a valuable resource for exploring these issues when they arise. As a trainee counsellor you may, often wisely, feel that in difficult situations it is best to focus on core skills such as paraphrasing, reflecting feelings, summarising and so on, but there is a risk of making the situation worse, e.g. summarising a depressed client's negative thoughts and feelings in a way which might lead them to feel even more depressed, or appearing to confirm a client's delusional thinking by paraphrasing it back to them. Experienced counsellors develop ways of responding with empathy whilst also gently and positively challenging. It is important not to seem to deny the client's experience or minimise the impact it may be having for them, but at the same time not to reinforce negative, irrational or otherwise problematic thoughts and behaviours.

An example of how to strive for such balance might be to respond with empathy to a client's depressed and negative feelings, whilst at the same time drawing attention to whatever efforts they are making to help themselves, for example by coming to talk to you about it. In a similar vein, if a client is experiencing hallucinations or delusional ideas, a useful starting point is often to acknowledge their experience and the emotional impact it seems to be having, whilst congruently stating that you do not share it. Focusing on the emotional impact of hallucinations or delusions can be productive if some level of insight is present in that it can reinforce the therapeutic relationship and lead to working on coping strategies.

Like all people, trainee counsellors can experience mental health problems, and indeed some of the challenges of training have the potential to contribute to difficulties. It is important to pay attention to your own well-being, both mental and physical, to take appropriate steps to look after yourself consistently and to address any difficulties when they arise. It may also be helpful to remind yourself that well-being is a continuum: you can expect to notice or suspect some 'symptoms' in yourself, especially when studying or working with mental health problems.

metaphors for counselling

▷ self-awareness

Metaphors can be very useful *in* counselling to help clarify an emotion or belief or reach an insight (Bayne and Thompson 2000; Bayne et al. 2008), and counsellors can help their clients explore a metaphor with open questions or what Tompkins et al. (2005) called 'clean language questions', like 'What strikes you about X?' and 'What might happen next?' Conversely, metaphors *for* counselling may help someone choose an orientation that suits them.

You may like to pause at this point and reflect on whether you currently have any metaphors for counselling (there are some suggestions later). What is counselling like? What is the nature of the counselling relationship?

One of our students used the following metaphor, which to us is *not* how we think anyone should see counselling! She described a series of interventions with a client as 'like playing a salmon' (i.e. with a fishing rod). It is difficult to see how this could be interpreted in any way that doesn't include the counsellor thinking she knows best and her being in control (quite apart from fish hooks).

The following metaphors include some which are quite often used for counselling, and some less familiar ones. What matters first is whether any of them feels promising or exactly right to you.

You may then wish to clarify it (perhaps with clean questions) or to relate it to counselling orientations. On the other hand, you may not find or create a metaphor that relates to you well enough.

Those metaphors you reject or find neutral can be just as helpful as those that you find appealing:

Companion	Healer
Adventurer	Warrior
Detective	Philosopher
Surgeon	Guide
Archaeologist	Terrier
Scientist	Midwife
Salesperson	Earth mother
Magician	

If you've been a client in counselling, you may also like to describe your counsellor or counsellors in this way. What effect is your counsellor's style or orientation having on your own style or choice of orientation? Another use of the list would be to explore fears and expectations of counsellor training.

mindfulness

▷ relaxation

Mindfulness is an approach to developing a more accepting, less judgemental awareness of your thoughts, feelings and actions in the present moment. It plays a central role in Buddhism, and has attracted a lot of interest among Western therapists as a means of alleviating anxiety and depression (Gunarata 2002; Segal et al. 2002; Hollon et al. 2006). A principle is that by observing inner reality more closely, one finds that happiness is not a quality brought about by a change in outer circumstances, but rather that it starts by releasing 'automatic' reactions toward pleasant and unpleasant situations or feelings. It has been successfully integrated with the principles of cognitive behaviour therapy by many practitioners (Segal et al. 2002; Crane 2008).

Mindfulness often involves the use of meditation techniques, but it can be practised in many aspects of life by focusing on connecting fully with – and experiencing in depth – whatever you are doing. Examples of meditation techniques and background information about mindfulness can be found at www.WiseBrain.org.

motives for becoming a counsellor

▷ choosing an orientation, good counsellors, self-awareness, strengths

Ideas about people's motives for becoming counsellors vary dramatically in how bleak or positive they are. We'll take a bleak example first. Persaud (1997) took the following list from Templer (1971). The 'types', which you may like to apply to yourself as an intending or trainee counsellor (but if you do, please remain open to the positive ideas to come), are:

- those with an uncertain sense of their identity;
- the socially inhibited or withdrawn;
- the dependent;
- those who like others to be dependent on them;
- the rigidly intellectual;
- the sadistic;
- those who have difficulty expressing hostility;
- the masochistic.

A more considered and balanced view was offered by Guy (1987), who distinguished between functional and dysfunctional motives. Examples of *functional* motives are having a natural interest in people and being emotionally insightful, i.e. in both cases, wanting to use and develop strengths. Guy's suggestions about *dysfunctional* motives are less shocking than those listed by Persaud, and he also qualifies them by seeing them as dysfunctional mainly in excess. For example, some experience of emotional pain may increase a person's capacity for empathy, but if the person is *greatly* preoccupied with healing that pain, it becomes a dysfunctional motive.

Similarly, Hawkins and Shohet (2006) see honest reflection as essential, and recommend 'facing the shadow' (p. 8). For example, they tell students and clients who thank them for good work that it is 'not us but themselves they should thank, yet secretly saying "… and me"' (p. 9). They later stress that 'It is not the needs themselves, but their denial that we believe can be so costly' (p. 13) and, conversely, that 'knowing ourselves, our motives and our needs, makes us more likely to be of real help' (p.14).

Corey and Corey (1998), too, see the same need or motive as having the potential to be positive or negative. They suggest asking yourself four questions about nine needs (pp. 4–7). The questions are:

1 Do I deny having certain needs?
2 How might I be able to satisfy both my own needs and those of the people who seek my help?
3 What needs of mine, if any, might I be inclined to meet at the expense of my clients?
4 Are some of my own needs so intense that they cannot be met?

In a later book, Corey (2005: 37) added a variation of one of these questions (to be asked frequently):

'Whose needs are being met in this relationship, my client's or my own?'

The focus therefore is on becoming *aware* of your needs and how they influence the quality of your relationship with others, especially clients. If you're not aware of a need, you're more likely to misuse other people to satisfy it. Corey and Corey's suggested needs are:

▸ to make an impact (related, for them, to power);
▸ to return a favour (e.g. by a teacher or therapist);
▸ to care for others (who cares for you?);
▸ for self-help;
▸ to be needed;
▸ for money;
▸ for prestige and status;
▸ to provide answers;
▸ for control.

The darker, dysfunctional or more dubious motives seem to us less prevalent than the positive ones and, where they do exist, to be more likely to be dominated by functional, positive ones.

Psychological type theory suggests the following core motives which, as with the earlier dark list, you may wish to try out for 'goodness of fit' on yourself, in your life generally, and in your work or possible work as a counsellor:

▸ for excitement and adventure;
▸ for autonomy;
▸ to be responsible and useful;
▸ to plan in detail;
▸ for stability and security;
▸ to develop new theories and ideas;
▸ to analyse;
▸ to become increasingly competent;
▸ for harmony;
▸ to develop yourself;
▸ to support other people.

multiculturalism

> ▷ **disability, diversity, gender**

The topic of multiculturalism, and the issues involved in making sure that clients from different cultural backgrounds are not discriminated against in terms of access to counselling or receiving an appropriate culturally sensitive service when they see a counsellor, have received a lot of attention in recent years. (See for example Lago 2005; Ridley 2005.) We are using the term 'culture' to relate to a broad range of factors which may include race, ethnicity, religion or spiritual beliefs, social background, sexuality, age, socioeconomic status, membership of identifiable groups or sub-groups etc. which tend to have a relationship to the individual's worldview, beliefs, values, attitudes, norms etc.

Some guidelines for working in a culturally sensitive way are:

1 Develop self-awareness of your 'personal culture' (see Diversity).
2 Try to avoid imposing your own values (consciously or unconsciously).
3 Recognise the limits of your ability to be empathic, genuine and accepting where there are cultural differences: discuss the consequences of this in supervision.
4 Regarding empathy:
   ‣ Don't pretend to understand if you don't.
   ‣ Seek clarification openly – ask the client to help you understand the influence of their cultural background.
   ‣ Encourage the client to ask you for clarification if they are not clear about the context in which you are speaking.
   ‣ Ask the client for examples to illustrate their experience – concrete examples may help you make sense of unfamiliar aspects of a different culture.
5 Talk about the dynamics of the relationship: how it is developing, how it feels, what is helpful, what is unhelpful, when etc. Ask the client to what extent they are getting what they want.

   The Ivey model for cultural empathy may be useful. It represents the various possible interactions between client, counsellor and their respective cultures:

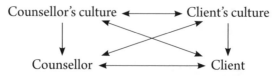

   The counsellor can usefully reflect on and explore the interactions of any of the above factors with the client (Ivey et al. 2008).
6 Do not stereotype clients – individuals vary within any group and these differences are often more important to the client.

7   Recognise that we all have multiple roles – the client is not defined by any one factor, cultural or otherwise, so avoid stereotyping.

8   Monitor any defensiveness on your part. It may arise from aspects of your own culture, or from a challenge to your self-perception as accepting, unbiased, non-discriminatory, without prejudice etc.

9   Exercise flexibility in planning and selecting interventions, and examine approaches used for cultural bias – are there implicit assumptions or values which may not be applicable to the client's culture?

10   Use approaches which best fit the client's strengths, resources, skills and preferences.

11   Do not try to protect clients from, or deny, emotional pain relating to oppression or discrimination.

m

n

non-verbal communication

> ▷ exercises, feedback, language and linguistics, room (counselling),
> self-awareness, skills training, video/DVD labs

Non-verbal communication (NVC) is relevant to some central aspects of counselling and therefore counsellor training, for example when a counsellor says something like 'I notice that I smiled when …', and when trainees are asked to observe and comment on the NVC in a counselling session. Observations might be made about eye contact, posture, voice quality and so on and you are likely to feel self-conscious doing this.

There is surprisingly little written about NVC and counselling, despite its central role in communication. However, it seems to be sufficient to distinguish kinds of NVC (partly as an aid to observation), to discuss interpreting NVC, and to clarify your views on aspects of NVC such as crying, touch, what counsellors wear and the room in which you counsel (Bayne et al. 2008).

notes, making

> ▷ critical thinking, plagiarism, reading as a skill, references in academic
> writing, study skills

For students, taking notes should be a creative activity. You are interacting with what the speaker says or with written material and taking out the relevant ideas and facts. Thus in some respects it is like the counselling skill of paraphrasing, but the emphasis is on testing how well you understand rather than on helping your client understand, and on your purpose (e.g. to contribute to an essay) rather than helping your client clarify their purpose.

Generally, it is most useful to put the other person's words into your own but sometimes they will put something so well that you'll decide to quote it. Accurate recording is an important academic value here – in the quote itself and in the reference for it.

For some, perhaps many, students, making marks on articles or books is a deep pleasure. It's perhaps partly a territorial claim, making the article or book more your own, but mainly it's actively working at understanding the ideas, facts, arguments etc. and choosing those that seem most relevant to your purpose in reading it: e.g. to write an essay or present a client in supervision. It is, of course, vandalism to mark books or journals which you do not own.

There are some specific techniques for making notes, e.g. the spider chart (Cottrell 2008). These suit some people very well and others not at all, and may be worth experimenting with.

notes during and after counselling sessions

▷ **boundaries, ethics**

Most counsellors do not take notes during counselling sessions. It can be perceived as a distraction by clients, who, naturally, may be curious about what you are writing. The act of writing at a particular point can convey the impression that something significant has just been said, yet it tends to take your attention away from the client and prevents you from seeming fully engaged with the relationship and the communication. On the other hand, some ways of working, for example some CBT techniques, can involve asking a lot of questions and gathering information which needs to be recorded and will be used, perhaps for homework, or referred back to in later sessions.

It may also be appropriate to take notes as you go during an assessment session, if the agency you are working for requires the completion of an assessment form. We suggest that in such cases it might be helpful to arrange things so that the client can see what you are writing and feel more involved in the process. Working across the corner of a desk is a possibility, or arranging chairs at right angles to each other with a coffee table in front. The taking of notes for specific reasons can then feel similar to other collaborative work you might do, such as brainstorming or an exercise such as the Lifeline (see entry above).

Counsellors have a responsibility to keep appropriate professional records of their work with clients. As a minimum this should include the time and duration of the session, some record of what was discussed, and any agreements or arrangements made. Counsellors vary in the amount of detail they record beyond this, but you should bear in mind that under data protection legislation the client can ask to see any notes that you keep, and that in the (unlikely) event of any legal proceedings taking place, your notes can be called for as evidence. (See Jenkins 2007 for clear guidance on this and other legal issues.)

It is therefore wise to keep your notes professional and write them in a style which you would be happy for the client to read, and which you would be able to defend in court if necessary. This might mean taking care to stick mainly to factual information about issues discussed, what was said and what was agreed. Care needs to be taken with drawing inferences, and recording any hunches or gut feelings. Opinions or conclusions need to be owned as such, stated tentatively, and linked to the evidence on which they are based.

You also have a responsibility to keep clients' notes safe and protect their confidentiality, and it is likely that your placement will have a policy in place for this which is in line with data protection law. Common practice is to keep notes in a locked filing cabinet which is fixed so that it cannot be removed from the premises, with the notes filed under a coding system and containing no reference to the client's name. The key to identify a particular client from their code is then kept in a separate locked location.

O

open circle

▷ **beginnings, self-awareness, trust**

The 'open circle' is one way of starting each day of your course. Its basic form is that, sitting in a circle, each person:

1 Talks about how they are or something that's happened or is going to happen – something personal – or says 'pass'.
2 Is fairly brief (usually up to about a minute).
3 Listens but does not comment on what anyone else says, either at the time or later. There is an exception to this guideline: sometimes someone says 'Like x, I feel ...' This is fine. The spirit of the guideline is to avoid evaluating, rescuing or empathising – at least not in words – and such links do not contradict this spirit, at least not usually or seriously.

This way of beginning has at least seven purposes. Four of these are obvious: it acts as a 'buffer' between the course and everything else; marking the transition may encourage some stabilising of mood – a little more calm, for example; it allows trainees and tutors to have some sense of how each person is today, and, in time, of their personalities and ways of being; and it is practice of self-disclosure (and possibly spontaneity) with some parallels with being a client.

Three other purposes are more subtle: each person can develop another aspect of their self-awareness by noticing their reactions to the others each week – emotions are stirred, biases can come into focus; it is intensive practice in hearing a variety of emotions without being overwhelmed and in being non-judgemental (accepting); and it is practice in *not* rescuing – at least in not expressing this anti-counselling reaction verbally. Not rescuing is part of being a good counsellor – in part because if a counsellor tries to help too many people there is less energy, time and focus for others.

The overall aim of the open circle is to help develop trust within the group. However, some trainees, either initially or persistently, find it difficult. The main objections that we've found are that it's very difficult to do, seems artificial, and, perhaps most of all, can be insensitive when someone is upset or angry.

For some people, the standard form of the open circle is a 'creeping threat'. As their turn approaches, their heart rate increases, their mouth gets dryer, their tension mounts. It can get easier, but is it worth it? Our reaction is to feel sympathetic but to see it as vital for trainees to understand and cope constructively with such reactions, especially when the benefits of the activity seem clear.

Is the open circle artificial? In a sense, counselling itself is artificial, but there is also within it an opportunity for real contact – and it works. An alternative would be to take a leisurely (more 'natural') approach to trust developing but the course would take longer and thus be less efficient: fewer counsellors, more expensively trained. (There is a similar tension between brief and open-ended counselling.) We have mixed feelings about the criterion of efficiency; it can have a cold-blooded feel to it, but it is also realistic, and in practice the open circle is often warm and trusting.

Is the open circle insensitive or even callous? The issue here is that keeping quiet after someone has said that they are upset or angry (say) can be seen as insensitive and uncaring. Moreover, sometimes there is a gulf between what one person says and what the next person says, e.g. 'I'm struggling with my mother's death and huge problems at work' and the next, 'I'm happy to have finished the essay.' We consider this to be the most problematic of the issues we have identified. It can be very hard not to speak, either in a positive way from a counselling point of view, e.g. with empathy, or a negative one, e.g. to attempt a rescue in a compulsive way. But the decisive principle is that it is important to practise not speaking in response to strong emotions or problems and to practise not automatically offering to help. Other parts of the course provide lots of opportunity to practise counselling responses.

Another problem that sometimes occurs is a student feeling impatient with others who are being less open than themselves – this is putting it gently (terms like 'drivel' and 'banal' have been used). You may like to consider possible responses by a tutor or yourself to this complaint.

Research on evaluations of the open circle

Students from eight of our course groups (163 people altogether) rated the elements of the rationale for the open circle and criticisms of it on nine scales, e.g.:

1 The open circle acts as a break or 'buffer' between the rest of my life and the course.

Not at all useful in this respect			Neutral			Very useful in this respect
1	2	3	4	5	6	7

We also asked for further comments and criticisms. The trainees were at different stages of their courses and their ratings were similar regardless of year or time of year (though only one of the groups was a second-year one).

All the purposes suggested were seen as achieved, though with a substantial neutral rating, typically by about a third of a group. The pattern of responses was similar for the criticisms: most trainees disagreed with all of them in a

proportion of three or four to one. 'Not at all true' was the most ticked response.
Examples of the further comments are:

> 'The group is far too large, I tend to feel tense, bored, frustrated, negative.'
> 'I feel a pressure to be entertaining, witty, interesting (pressure of my own making).'
> 'I feel silently judged.'
> 'I *plan* what to say and is that useful?'
> 'I tend to keep it light.'
> 'Useful to think, during the week, "Shall I say this?"'
> 'Helps to take on board fairly quickly where people are "at".'
> 'It's a magic space.'
> 'Just because it's artificial doesn't mean it's bad!'
> 'More like a bridge.'
> 'Helps to bond us as a group.'
> 'Opportunity to practise not being shy.'
> 'Hard to not ask people later.'
> 'I get bored. Some people talk too long.'
> 'Often consoles me that I'm not alone in my anxieties.'
> 'Breathing space.'

Variations

One group was concerned about the disruptive effects of people arriving late.
After discussing various options, including late arrivals waiting outside until the
end of the circle, the group decided to leave empty chairs near the door and
agreed that anyone speaking would pause to allow the late person to sit down.
This was seen as the best balance of respect for everyone's needs and rights.

Several variations of the basic format are possible. For example, people can
either speak in order of seating – going round the circle – or when they want to
(including to say 'pass'). In the first of these options, anyone can speak first and
then say who's next (and therefore who's last). Other variations are to specify
the content, e.g. emotions only, or a positive experience, or to use a variation of
the Gestalt technique 'Now I am aware of …'

In addition, the open circle can also be used to end a session, a day or a
weekend. Here the purposes are largely the same but with some degree of
'closure' or 'unfinished business' as well, or a focus forward: what might I try
doing differently as a result of today?

p

panicky, feeling

▷ de-skilled, distressed, expectations, failing, fears, stress

personal development

▷ assertiveness, journal, lifeline exercise, motives, open circle, personal therapy, personality theory, self-awareness

Personal development is a central aspect of counsellor training and a life-long process for counsellors. Alongside acquiring the knowledge and skills needed to work effectively with clients, you also need to be developing self-awareness; an ability to reflect on and make use of your experience; robustness in coping with emotional demands; the skills and qualities needed to form and sustain helping relationships with diverse clients; and the abilities to critically evaluate your work, elicit and use feedback from others, and recognise the need for personal and professional support. For thoughtful discussions of some of the issues in designing personal development training, see Wilkins (1997) and Spencer (2006).

We encourage a broad view of what constitutes personal development. For example, you may have read a novel or seen a film which you found particularly moving, inspiring or disturbing; undertaken a particular challenge, experienced something new, or achieved something significant; found yourself in an unfamiliar role, be experiencing a relationship in an unaccustomed way, or found a particular communication or interaction thought-provoking or moving. In all of these examples, and many more, it may be possible to identify some new learning or insight about yourself, your impact on others, or their impact on you. This in turn can help you recognise new resources or areas for development and action.

personal development groups

▷ experiential groups, personal development

personal therapy

> ▷ choosing a counsellor, evidence-based practice, personal development,
> self-awareness

There is marked disagreement among counsellors and counsellor trainers about how necessary it is for trainee counsellors to have their own counselling as part of their training. Psychodynamic courses generally require trainees to have (extensive) personal therapy, other approaches may require it or strongly recommend it, and some regard it as optional, encouraging trainees to be clients if they need to be in order to explore a particular problem, or if they choose that route to developing their self-awareness.

The research evidence on the value of personal therapy for trainees is mixed (Grimmer 2005; Norcross 2005; Daw and Joseph 2007). For example, Grimmer concluded that 'organisations that rely on empirically-based research will continue to point to the lack of evidence for the effectiveness of personal therapy in enhancing outcomes and those who believe in clinical wisdom will continue to insist on it' (2005: 40).

If other reasons for choosing a course have been decisive, you may decide to tolerate personal therapy that you regard as unnecessary. Alternatively, you may feel enthusiastic about it as a requirement – or confused or ambivalent. The following arguments may help you clarify your view, or challenge it.

The arguments *for* personal therapy include:

- increased self-awareness;
- help in coping with the particular stress of counsellor training (as well as other stress);
- direct experience of being a client.

The arguments *against* include:

- the possibility of other ways of increasing self-awareness;
- the cost, which has implications for who can afford training;
- the fact that some trainees have already been clients;
- the sense that *requiring* counselling seems contradictory (and possibly unethical).

personality theory

> ▷ choosing a counselling orientation, motives, psychological type,
> self-awareness

There is surprisingly little material on individual differences in personality in the counselling literature. As Feltham and Dryden (2006: 73) put it (and temperament and personality mean the same thing in this context): 'Client temperament is an important area, often overlooked or not well understood by counsellors.' There is some overlap between theories of counselling and theories of personality but the emphasis tends to be on the theory's assumptions (which may be treated as truths) about human nature and personality in general.

However, more work on individual differences and their implications for counselling is beginning to appear (Provost 1993; Bayne 2004; Singer 2005) and the two personality theories which may be most promising, partly because they explain and potentially integrate other theories, are McAdams' three levels model and the 16 personality types of psychological type theory in its Myers–Briggs Type Indicator (MBTI) sense (see entry on Psychological type theory).

McAdams' (e.g. 1995) levels are:

1 Traits, e.g. warm, anxious.
2 Personal concerns and characteristic adaptations.
3 Integrative life stories.

To know a person well is to know them at all three levels. The underlying idea is that counselling is more likely to be effective if the client is known at one or more of the levels.

In counsellor training, one use of McAdams' model is as a response to trainees who dismiss the idea and value of traits. It can help to reframe objections like 'I vary', 'I don't like being put in a box', and 'There's a lot more to me than these test results'.

The broader case for including personality theory in its individual difference sense in counsellor training is threefold. First, as indicated above, it is directly relevant to such questions as: Do some forms of counselling suit some people (of particular personalities) more than others? Do some counsellors (of particular personalities) suit some clients more than others? Do some techniques? Do some ways of introducing or using techniques? Conversely, for all these questions, are some combinations significantly less likely to be effective? Second, personality theories, especially those well supported by research, are directly relevant to some central elements of self-awareness. Third, there are implications for how much change is possible in certain respects: major personality characteristics are stable by definition. These implications are relevant to clients and also to counsellor training itself, and to selection for counsellor training.

placement, finding a

▷ application forms, rejection, room (counselling), selection procedures

BACP accredited training courses have to include a supervised practice placement. At the time of writing this needs to encompass at least 100 hours of client work, but the minimum is likely to be increased shortly to 150 hours of client work plus 50 hours of additional work-based learning.

Looking for a placement can be frustrating and demoralising. Your tutors will give you some guidance on when you should begin trying to secure a placement – sometimes this will be during the first year, after you have been assessed as competent to see clients, and sometimes it will be the second year. Your course will have some resources to help with the process: contact details and information about organisations where students have been on placement previously, or which have made contact to offer placements.

You may also learn about potential placements from former students or other contacts, or by investigating counselling services offered in your local area and approaching the providers. Community centres, volunteer bureaux and local press may be useful sources of information about services available. In some areas, there is a lot of competition for placement opportunities, so you should pursue a range of possibilities. With luck this will also mean that you are able to exercise some choice about which placement you accept.

Give some thought to what kind of placement would suit you best. Do you want to work with a particular client group (in terms of age, gender, section of the community, presenting issue etc.), or do you want more generic experience? Do you want to aim for the health service, voluntary or charitable sector, or a private agency? You may want to vary your experience by taking on more than one placement during your training, if the opportunity arises and you have time.

Selection procedures vary. You might make initial contact by phone or email, and may be able to arrange an informal visit. It is important to have prepared a good CV, which highlights your relevant experience. This should include previous experience in any capacity with the potential client group; experience of counselling or using counselling skills; and other relevant experience in the helping field or in working with people generally. You need to provide evidence that you have the skills and qualities to develop as a counsellor, that you will be reliable and professional in your dealings with clients, that you will be able to work with the systems in place for assessment, referral, record keeping and so on, and that you have reached a basic level of competence in order to be able to work safely with the client group. If your CV creates a favourable impression, you are then likely to be called for an interview. It helps to gather as much information as you can about the organisation in preparation for this. Marketing leaflets, websites, former students and your tutors may be able to help.

If you are successful, you will then have to decide whether to accept the placement. A number of factors need to be in place to make it a satisfactory and safe experience, including adequate resources and support, and systems for assessment and referral. The following checklist may be useful:

Key

Column 1:   ✓ = adequate/yes,

? = needs to be checked, or

✗ = not adequate

Column 2:   Please indicate action and by whom

	1	2
1 Suitability of counselling rooms ‣ Types and arrangement of seating ‣ Other furniture/objects in the room ‣ Lighting and decor ‣ Private and free from disturbance and noise ‣ Overall suitable for counselling		
2 Personal safety ‣ Availability of alarm system/panic button and/or other security arrangements ‣ Written procedures for dealing with critical incidents/risk of aggressive/violent behaviour by clients or others ‣ Availability of other people in the building while student is seeing clients ‣ Student knows how to identify indicators and how to deal with critical incidents and aggressive/violent behaviour by clients or others		
3 Client reception ‣ Suitability of reception procedures ‣ Suitability of waiting areas		
4 Allocation of clients to students ‣ Satisfactory procedures for the assessment/allocation of suitable clients to students ‣ Availability and use of any referral information		
5 Information for clients ‣ Clients are given accurate information on the nature of the service being offered and type of contract ‣ Clients are informed about the experience/qualification/status of the student		
6 Confidentiality ‣ Student is aware of BACP/BPS agency/organisation codes/policy on confidentiality		

7 Insurance ‣ Agency/organisation has Pubic Liability Policy which covers the student and clients ‣ Student has personal/professional indemnity insurance (and/or is aware of BACP/BPS and agency policy/guidelines)		
8 Domiciliary visits ‣ Students are not normally permitted to undertake home visits (unless part of their paid employment contract)		
9 Responsibility ‣ Appropriately qualified/experienced person has clinical responsibility for student's work ‣ Quality of student's work is monitored and managed		

Some students develop a sense of urgency and a lot of anxiety about securing a placement, and while it is clearly a central part of your training, we advise you not to panic if you don't find one quickly. Remember that the further you progress into your training course, the better you look to a potential placement. In particular, some placements will only accept second-year students, so the number of opportunities available to you is likely to increase considerably once you have completed the first year.

Completing a hundred or more client hours in a year can be a challenge if there are a lot of demands on your time but it is well within the bounds of what can be achieved. In any case, training courses are aware that finding opportunities for client work has become more difficult over recent years and will have arrangements in place to allow you to complete outstanding hours beyond the end of the taught programme. Your course handbook should include information on this.

placement, managing your

▷ **assertiveness, boundaries**

Managing your placement is made simpler by making sure that appropriate arrangements are in place from the start, that you understand what is expected of you and what you can expect from the placement, and that lines of communication are clear. Below is an example of a placement registration document which addresses a number of these areas, and sets up a three-way contract between the placement provider, the trainee counsellor and the training organisation:

ARRANGEMENTS FOR CLIENT WORK (at the agency/organisation)

1   Number of client hours per week:
2   When will they be seen?
3   Where will they be seen?
4   Arrangements for case notes/records:
5   Which Code of Ethics and Practice does the agency/organisation abide by? (Please circle)
     BACP/BPS/OTHER (please specify)
6   To whom is the student primarily accountable
     (a) for her/his clinical work?
     (b) for routine management/organisation?
7   Who conducts the initial assessment of the client?
8   What is (if any) the theoretical orientation of the agency/organisation?
9   Does the agency/organisation hold a public liability insurance that covers the student and his/her clients? YES/NO
10   Does the agency/organisation have a written health and safety policy which covers the following:
     (a) Procedures for dealing with critical incidents, including situations involving violent and/or aggressive clients or other visitors? YES/NO
     (b) Procedures for identifying clients at risk to themselves or others? YES/NO
   Will the student be given a copy of the policy or told where it can be found? YES/NO

AGENCY/ORGANISATIONAL REQUIREMENTS
(e.g. rules or requirements regarding confidentiality, audio-tape recording clients, attendance at meetings, theoretical orientation, security arrangements and any other limitations or constraints.) Please continue, if necessary, on a separate sheet.

ARRANGEMENTS FOR COUNSELLING SUPERVISION
Is counselling supervision provided by the agency/organisation? YES/NO
If YES,
1   Who offers the supervision?
2   Type (please circle): INDIVIDUAL/GROUP/OTHER (please specify)
3   Frequency (e.g. weekly, fortnightly etc.):
If NO,
1   Is the student expected to organise his/her own external clinical supervision? YES/NO
2   Does the agency/organisation monitor external supervision? YES/NO
3   Does (or will) the agency/organisation have any contract with the external supervisor? YES/NO
4   Who has clinical responsibility for the student's counselling?

COURSE SUPERVISION
Details of any supervision offered as part of the course:

The course will respect and/or adhere to all agency/organisational requirements (limitations, constraint rules and procedures). Confidentiality will be strictly observed.

ARRANGEMENTS FOR DEALING WITH ISSUES/COMPLAINTS
The agency/organisation contact person is asked to contact, in the first instance, the Course Director concerning:
(a) further information about the course, liaison and communication issues;
(b) any complaints against the student for unprofessional, unethical or incompetent work with clients or agency/organisation staff;
(c) any recommended further training needs for the student.

PLACEMENT CONTRACT
Length of contract:

Start date: .... Finishing date: ....

Signatories to this contract:

1   **For the agency/organisation:**
    I confirm that the agency/organisation will provide client work opportunities/ placement for this student and that the details on this form about the agency/organisation are correct, to the best of my knowledge. The agency/ organisation accepts the arrangements for course supervision and for dealing with issues and complaints.

    NAME: .... SIGNATURE: ....

    DATE: ....

2   **For the course:** [Course clinical supervisor or course leader]
    I approve this client work opportunity/placement and agree to the agency/ organisation requirements. I confirm that the course staff will adhere to the BACP Ethical Framework.

    NAME: .... SIGNATURE: ....

    DATE: ....

3   **The student:**
    I confirm that I will adhere to the BACP Ethical Framework and that I accept the agency/organisation requirements.

    NAME: .... SIGNATURE: ....

    DATE: ....

NB This form is to be kept in the student's Professional Log. The student should give a copy of the completed form to the agency/organisation contact person.

p

You should be allocated a co-ordinator or mentor at the placement who will be your main point of contact and will arrange your induction. Make sure that you become familiar with the policies of the placement organisation regarding assessment, referral, record keeping, confidentiality, supervision, clinical responsibility, health and safety, risk management and so on.

Hopefully, things will then run smoothly: you will be allocated suitable clients and begin to accumulate your hours. Problems do occasionally arise: examples can include lack of clients, confused administrative arrangements, allocation of inappropriate clients, inadequate security arrangements or lack of support. In the first instance you should discuss any concerns with your placement co-ordinator. If this does not resolve the situation, you should then discuss your difficulties with your tutor, who may suggest a three-way meeting with the placement co-ordinator. Occasionally a resolution is not possible and a trainee might decide to end a placement and find an alternative, but this is rare.

A similar process should occur if the placement co-ordinator has concerns about your conduct or practice – the co-ordinator (or supervisor) will discuss them with you in the hope that things can be resolved. If not, they may wish to arrange to meet with you and your tutor to discuss the way forward. Occasionally a placement may have to be suspended or terminated, and your tutor will explore the implications of this with you.

In most cases, however, management of the placement is a matter of good communication: about where you are with your clients, when you have space for another client and so on. There are likely to be evaluation/report forms to complete for your training course and you should make sure you get these in good time and make arrangements for the relevant people at your placement (co-ordinator, supervisor) to discuss them with you and fill in their sections.

Ending your placement needs to be handled sensitively. You may choose to continue with it after the end of your training course, but if not, you should work out a plan for ending with your clients or for referring them to other counsellors.

plagiarism

> ▷ assessment of coursework (issues), critical thinking, notes (making),
> references (academic), writing (academic)

Plagiarism is pretending that someone else's work – ideas, words or creations – is your own. In its most extreme form, it is, for example, paying someone to write a piece of coursework for you. Copying sections from articles or books without referencing them is also plagiarism, though a problem here is that many published authors 'borrow' ideas, words and phrases from others but put them together with their own thoughts in new and individual ways, so where does 'creative borrowing' end and plagiarism (cheating) begin? And what about other people commenting on a draft?

Another problem is to decide on the most effective approach to reducing plagiarism. Is it to use powerful electronic detection techniques in a kind of arms race, or is a preventive approach better? Counselling courses are probably more likely to take a preventive approach, helped by the personal element in much of the coursework. For example, two of our essays ask students to respectively apply a theory of personality to themselves and a model of loss to a personal transition, e.g. an illness or the end of relationship. The student also evaluates the theory both in itself and for its value or not in making sense of their personality or transition. It thus has both personal and academic elements, and the personal element would be harder, though not impossible, to plagiarise. This is also an argument against anonymous marking on counselling courses (not that this is very practical anyway).

Plagiarism may also be reduced or prevented through positive perspectives, e.g. by emphasising the value of putting ideas into your own words (the consumer metaphor for the role of student is a force against this) and the integrity of acknowledging others' contributions, e.g. 'There seem to be three possible reasons for X, two of them suggested by Smith (2007). Smith argued ...'

The smaller course groups typical of counselling courses are probably also a factor. Tutors are more likely to notice differences in writing style between different pieces of work (though students not putting their names on their work, intended to reduce bias in assessment, may have the opposite effect). Many universities have policy statements about plagiarism on their websites, including preventive strategies and penalties for offences. The Plagiarism Advisory Service is another useful source.

presentations, making

▷ assertiveness, essays and reports, imagery, relaxation, selection interviews, supervision

You are very likely to make presentations during training, either in a small supervision group or to the whole group. This can be daunting. Many people, including many famous people, are afraid of public speaking and have been coached by specialists (Rodenburg 2007).

They are recommended, for example, to prepare for a presentation by observing their surroundings (to become more alert and engaged), to relax (especially their shoulders and breathing), to vary their tone, to use pauses, to use imagery, to drink water, to say phrases like 'Ningy, Nongy, Noo' many times (to exercise their lips, tongue etc.).

Another aspect of preparation is also widely recommended: to think about your audience (empathy, in a sense), and what you want them to know or be able to do as a result of your presentation. Then work within a structure such as the following:

1 State your position.
2 Give reasons.
3 Give examples.
4 Summarise.

Or:

1 State the problem.
2 State the effects.
3 Suggest solutions.

Good counselling overlaps in some respects with making presentations, e.g. use of silence, 'contact' with your audience/client, trusting yourself to find the words (if, as usually advised, you've prepared points rather than sentences).

process reports, writing

▷ **critical thinking, language, non-verbal communication, transcripts**

A process report is an analysis of an example of your counselling. This will usually be based on an extract from a recorded session, often around 15 to 20 minutes long. You will probably be required to produce a transcript of the chosen extract, and to base your analysis on it. As usual, make sure you are clear about the criteria for the assessment so that you can choose an extract which best demonstrates the skills and qualities required.

The purpose of a process report is to demonstrate that you can reflect on and evaluate your practice realistically and in detail, showing awareness of the qualities and skills used, and the therapeutic process taking place between you and the client. You will usually need to focus on two areas: evaluating specific skills and interventions, and analysing the underlying processes and therapeutic relationship.

In relation to specific skills and interventions, a useful structure to consider is:

▸ *Intention*: What was your rationale for a particular intervention? What were you hoping to achieve by it?
▸ *Impact*: What was actually the result of the intervention? How did the client respond (both verbally and non-verbally)?
▸ *Alternatives*: With hindsight, what alternative interventions might you have used? What would have been the likely impact?

As well as providing a detailed evaluation of specific interventions, you also need to demonstrate your awareness of the underlying and evolving processes taking place in the session. Some useful questions to consider are:

- How well did you demonstrate the core conditions of empathy, acceptance and congruence during this extract? How did the client respond to this?
- To what extent were you aware of the client's agenda for the session? How was this communicated?
- What specific approaches, models or techniques were you using and how effective were you in this?
- What progress or forward movement is evident during the session?
- What impact were you having on the client and what impact were they having on you?
- Were there any key points when the dynamic of the relationship changed?
- What feelings did you experience at different points during the session and how did you manage or use them?
- What issues or questions were raised for you during the session?

In responding to these questions, you should look for evidence from the transcript to support what you want to say. Remember that a process report is an analysis and evaluation of your work, and should explore both the strengths and the areas for development that are in evidence. You should aim for a balance – do not be overly self-critical on the one hand, nor defensive and self-justifying on the other.

professional log

> ▷ case studies, notes (counselling sessions), process reports

Most training courses will require you to keep a professional log. This is an ongoing record of your practice and development, which will be added to continuously during your course; it will be assessed at the end, and perhaps at one or more points along the way. The intention is to develop good practice in keeping appropriate records of your professional activities, which you will need to do in the future for the purposes of gaining and maintaining professional accreditation.

Exactly what is required in a professional log varies from course to course, but the following are examples of what is often required:

- *Records of your client work*
  - ▷ Details of your placement, including any checklists, contract etc.
  - ▷ A log of client hours including brief details such as date, time, duration, client code, session number, issues discussed.
  - ▷ More detailed analysis of a specified number of client sessions.
  - ▷ Placement reports.
- *Records of supervision*
  - ▷ Details of your supervisor(s), contract etc.
  - ▷ A log of the supervision you have received, including date, time, duration, supervisor, issues discussed.

- ▷ More detailed reflection on a specified number of supervision sessions.
- ▷ Supervisor reports.
- ‣ *Records of personal/professional development*
  - ▷ A log of personal and professional development activities, which might include personal therapy, other courses or workshops attended, support or personal development groups, significant reading etc.
  - ▷ More detailed reflections on a sample of the above activities.
- ‣ A *self-appraisal report* where you reflect on your progress/development in the above areas, identify your strengths and areas for development, set goals and plan actions for the future.

On your particular course you may be required to include other items in your log, for example records of your skills practice sessions and feedback, evidence of addressing issues relating to the ethical framework or diversity and equality etc.

We suggest writing your log each week. If you allow yourself to fall behind, getting up to date can be very daunting. In addition, many items in the log require you to reflect on specific experiences with clients, supervisors etc., and this is best done soon after they happen. Trying to reconstruct a counselling or supervision session from memory long after the event is very difficult and less likely to lead to insight or learning.

psychological type (MBTI) theory

> ▷ **personality theory, self-awareness, strengths**

The MBTI (Myers–Briggs Type Indicator) is the most widely used non-clinical measure of personality, and has been for more than 20 years. Over 2 million MBTI questionnaires, in 21 languages, are completed each year. It is used primarily to improve individual and team performance. It is also used to help people cope with stress (including reducing boredom through finding true interests), in career development, to reduce conflict, to improve leadership skills and time management.

Underlying these uses are two general aims:

1 To increase people's understanding and appreciation of some of their main strengths and potential strengths, and their core motives. It can also explain conflicts between different parts of the same personality.
2 To increase people's understanding and appreciation of the strengths, potential strengths and core motives of other people. This goes beyond just tolerating the whole range of people's natural strengths – 'it takes all sorts' – to a different mindset which values the differences. Thus, it takes an abstract ideal and makes it practical, counteracting the human tendency to judge people who are different as stupid, inefficient, awkward or mad.

The MBTI is widely used for several reasons:

- It uses positive and constructive language. There are no bad types.
- It has an extensive research base. The free, online MBTI bibliography at www.capt.org has more than 10,000 references. Much of the research on the 'Big Five' approach to personality, which dominates academic psychology, also supports the validity of the MBTI.
- It is very versatile in its range of applications and in the levels of sophistication at which it can be applied.

There are four pairs of preferences:

Extraversion (E)	or	Introversion (I)
Sensing (S)	or	Intuition (N)
Thinking (T)	or	Feeling (F)
Judging (J)	or	Perceiving (P)

The meaning of each preference is indicated in Table 3.

Table 3   *Characteristics associated with each preference*

E More outgoing and active	**I** More reflective and reserved
S More practical and interested in facts and details	**N** More interested in possibilities and an overview
T More logical and reasoned	**F** More agreeable and appreciative
J More planning and coming to conclusions	**P** More easy-going and flexible

Psychological type theory's relevance to counsellor training is illustrated in several entries, e.g. those on Decisions, Good counsellors, Stress, and Time management. Bayne (2004) is a general introduction, Tieger and Barron-Tieger (2000, 2007) review applications to relationships and careers respectively, and Provost (1993) discusses case studies of her counselling clients of each 'type'.

p

q

qualifications, academic

▷ **critical thinking, experience, good counsellors, strengths**

Courses vary in how open they are to selecting people with no academic qualifications. Some have an explicit policy of considering such 'non-traditional' applicants but usually – and reasonably – ask for evidence of the ability to study at the level of the course. For a postgraduate course, this would mean something you'd written, perhaps a report at work or an article, or a full personal statement in the application form – anything that shows critical thinking (and other qualities and skills). Critical thinking can, of course, be shown at interview too, but first it is necessary to be offered an interview!

Our experience, in a university with an explicit goal and history of supporting non-traditional students, is that it can be deeply rewarding for the students and us to do so. Two contrasting examples both illustrate this.

The first is fairly straightforward: X left school at 15, though in a sense was hardly ever there, and when she applied to us in her mid-thirties was running a small business, read widely (including academic books), and showed in her application she'd thought about them and had been influenced by them.

In contrast, Y was a dental assistant in her early twenties: age, academic qualifications, experience (not even a short course on counselling skills) were all against her, and so was her spelling and grammar. And yet she conveyed a sense of self and language in her application that 'worked', and she did the same in her interviews. We asked her to work on her writing skills before she came on the course, and, in the course itself, she needed a lot of feedback on her written work, but the qualities we'd observed were real. She passed the course and contributed well to the course group. She subsequently passed an MA in Counselling at another university.

r

race

▷ **multiculturalism**

readiness to begin training

▷ **personal development, self-awareness, stress**

In order to begin training as a counsellor, you need to have reached a certain level in terms of maturity, self-awareness, personal development etc. The BACP criteria for training courses (BACP 2009a) suggest the following:

- Self-awareness, maturity and stability
- Ability to make use of and reflect upon life experience
- Capacity to cope with the emotional demands of the course
- Ability to cope with the intellectual and academic requirements
- Ability to form a helping relationship
- Ability to be self-critical and use both positive and negative feedback
- Awareness of the nature of prejudice and oppression
- Awareness of issues of difference and equality
- Ability to recognise the need for personal and professional support
- Competence in generic skills including: literacy, numeracy, information technology, administrative skills, self-management skills, communication and interpersonal skills
- Commitment to self-development.

You may find it useful to review this list in relation to yourself, and to look for evidence which indicates your readiness on each criterion. If you find it difficult to do so in relation to some of the criteria, this may be an indication that there is more work to do to prepare yourself for training, and a guide as to what kinds of experiences might be useful. You could also ask others for their views.

r

reading as a skill

▷ **critical thinking, notes (making), writing (expressive)**

'The literature can be a place of irrelevance, illusion and even of danger.' (McLeod 1997: 162)

McLeod (1997) argued for the benefits of reading widely about counselling too, in order to develop the ability to make conceptual links and apply ideas, and to encourage a sense of inquiry, for example, both of these being 'higher level cognitive skills that play a significant role in therapy practice' (p. 156). His view of the potential disadvantages of reading widely about counselling included the fact that 'the dominant voice is male, white, heterosexual, able-bodied' (p. 153) and that it is also largely 'logical, rational, linear, scientific' (p. 162) when therapy itself is multilayered and ambiguous.

In our view a further problem is that some writing on counselling (and other subjects) is empty generalities or just unintelligible. Wheen (2004) is an effective critic of such writing, taking particular pleasure in savaging certain writers on structuralism and postmodernism: 'One can gaze at this paragraph for hours and be none the wiser' (p. 88).

Wheen described an experiment by Sokal, a physics professor who tested intellectual standards in postmodernism by submitting a nonsensical article entitled 'Transgressing the boundaries: toward a transformative hermeneutics of quantum gravity' to a leading US journal of cultural studies. It was accepted and a week after its publication Sokal revealed the hoax and his motives (primarily to challenge the intellectual worth of postmodernism). As Wheen points out, attempts to reply were hampered by Sokal's use of numerous genuine quotations in his spoof article.

We suggest, then, that if you don't like a book or article, or don't understand it, consider not reading it. There is a point where 'reader's block' is justified or where persistence stops being a good quality.

There are detailed analyses of the skills of reading (Cottrell 2008) and nothing shameful about needing to develop one or more of these skills, or at least experimenting with them to find those that work for you. The techniques exist and can be learned. For example, one approach (which will be too mechanical for some tastes but may nevertheless describe what skilful readers of scientific literature often do) is the 'light survey' of a book. Essentially, the light survey is to read the chapter headings first as an indication of the main themes and how the author develops them, then the first and last chapters. At this point you have a good sense of the book and decide whether or not to continue. If you continue, read the first and last paragraphs of the other chapters. Then, again decide whether or not to continue. Thus far this method makes some sense to us; the next recommended steps less so: they are to survey the index, reread the chapter headings, and then any relevant sections of the rest of the book (Oleson and Arkin 2006).

Similarly, with articles reporting research, read the Abstract first, then the first few paragraphs of the Introduction, then the first paragraph or two of the Discussion (which usually summarise the results). That's enough to decide whether the article is relevant to your purpose, and to decide whether you need to read the Method section carefully, for example. Oleson and Arkin (2006) also recommend the 'good trick' of reading the first sentence of each paragraph.

A key idea about reading is that there are many different styles, e.g. skim, depth, immersion, critical, fun. Each of these will be best for a particular person, purpose and book, article, blog etc., but flexibility and option do seem desirable. However, while it seems to us to be a good thing to be able to both immerse ourselves in a novel and to skim many links on the internet, overuse of one method may tend to make using the others more difficult.

reading lists

> reading as a skill

It is not usually feasible to read all or even most of the books and articles on a typical reading list, nor is it intended that you should. Rather, the list makes suggestions (and to some extent offers alternatives) and the idea is that you try some of them, looking for ideas and a writing style that engages, stimulates and stretches you – or, at least, that you're not overawed or baffled by. Where 'core' texts are identified, these are obviously the recommended place to start.

references for applications

> experience

Nearly all courses and jobs ask for references but in their usual form they're largely pointless (Dobson 1989; Aamodt 2001, 2007; Nicklin and Roch 2009). This is partly because they're nearly always very positive and partly because they can say more about the writer (their favourite terms for describing personality, their values and biases) than about the applicant or candidate. Another factor is fear of being sued for damages. Indeed, some organisations now provide very minimal references as a preventative step, e.g. 'X worked here between these dates'.

Nevertheless, you are very likely to be asked to give the names and addresses of two or more referees. This can be a problem, especially if you have not been in paid employment or have been a student for many years, but you can state this fact and difficulty clearly in your application. It's also sensible, and polite, to check with potential referees that they're willing to write a reference for you, and to update them briefly on your experience, motives and aspirations.

references in academic writing

> critical thinking, plagiarism, reading

Academic writing includes reading in a focused and discriminating way, and citing the sources you find useful. Citing references has two main purposes: it acknowledges the contribution of others and it helps readers know where they can read further about something of particular interest to them. It also shows whoever is marking your essay how well you've found and used helpful sources.

If your course is at a university, the library will probably have a detailed guide on how to cite references. We've used the Harvard system in this book, and it is clearly outlined (14 pages) on the University of East London (UEL) website. Go to Library, then Referencing. Unusual forms of citation are included, e.g. films, TV programmes, photography, e-books and electronic discussion groups and bulletin boards.

Brief quotations can be very effective, and the page number should be included for the reasons noted earlier.

referral

▷ assessment, failing, loss

rejection for a course or placement

▷ choosing a career, failing, loss, stress, support

The most likely explanation for your application for a course or placement being rejected is that there were more suitable applicants than places. The selectors know this and hopefully say it at some point in their selection procedures, but it is harder for the applicants to believe it: they haven't seen the piles of application forms or realise how little can separate those put in the 'probably interview' or 'definitely interview' categories rather than the 'reject'. Worse, if you ask the selectors what influenced their decision (as some researchers have done), they may be able to say something plausible and rational, but is it the real reason?

This picture has several implications for applicants and for selectors. For applicants, it means making your form individual, and considering showing it to friends or colleagues who can give you informed feedback. And, if you were rejected after interview, you could try to see it – though this may seem absurdly resilient – as interviewing practice which gives you much to analyse and reflect on. It also means taking the explanation offered above seriously rather than believing that you are inadequate in this respect (or that the selectors or their selection procedures are), though all these explanations may be true too.

Another implication for rejected applicants is that it may be worth persisting. We are surprised by how few rejected applicants apply again (though they may have been accepted for another course). We have accepted about half of those who reapplied.

A final issue for rejected applicants is whether or not to ask for feedback from the selectors. There are practical and ethical problems here. The practical problem is alluded to above: the selectors may not know or it may be primarily or only a matter of chance. Moreover, to give feedback well takes time and energy, which, from the selectors' point of view, is better used on teaching and other activities. The ethical difficulties of giving feedback to rejected applicants are illustrated in the following example.

Suppose that the selectors assess an applicant as too emotionally unstable or narcissistic (qualities which are probably not positively correlated with effectiveness as a counsellor), saying or writing this to an applicant is problematic. First, the judgement may be wrong. Second, the evidence for it may well be open to other interpretations or to challenge and protest, and argument may ensue. Third, feedback of such a personal and sensitive nature is most ethically given in a therapy relationship or as part of an assessment or development centre. It needs to be done carefully and probably gently, and would need far more time than is justified. The selector is not acting as a therapist with applicants.

Organisations are not at present (2009) obliged by English law to give reasons for rejecting applicants and many choose not to do so or to be very bland. There is empirical support for this position, e.g. Schinkel et al. (2004) found that detailed feedback was more upsetting than a straightforward rejection. However, their study was a simulation rather than a study of applicants who'd really been rejected and it was, as the authors recognise, only one study.

For selectors, there are two implications of our discussion of rejection. One is to realise (probably remember) how painful rejection is and how insecure and inadequate those rejected can feel. The other is to be as systematic and fair as possible in how we rate application forms and interviewees. For some selectors this means using rating scales and sometimes weighting some criteria more than others. For others, such complexity is an attempt to camouflage an intrinsically flawed and subtle procedure in which luck plays a major part.

relationships with friends, family and work colleagues, effects of counsellor training on

▷ assertiveness, boundaries, criticisms of counselling, stress

There is some evidence that counsellor training can bring about significant changes in trainees. Indeed, we hope so. However, Dexter (1996), in a study involving 34 trainees, cautions that the changes may be so profound that courses should offer more information about the extent of personal change which is likely and that, arguably, informed consent should be sought. 'The findings reveal significant change across the domains of thinking, attitudes and behaviour, and it is suggested that these changes may have a powerful effect upon the conduct of the subjects' lives' (p. 230).

Dexter's findings suggest a number of positive changes, such as increased levels of skill and confidence and an increase in unconditional positive regard for self. However, they also indicate some potentially difficult or negative changes in attitudes towards family, such as family being associated with stasis, and relationships with family being less confident, less comfortable and less trusting. Similarly, Truell (2001) found 'considerable disruption' (p. 65) of relationships in a small interview study of six recent graduates from a UK Counselling Diploma (orientation not specified, ages 25–43, four females, two males): his participants all reported having fewer friends than before their course, and five had 'experienced difficulties' with their partners (though five also reported better relationships than before their training). For two participants, the difficulties lasted 18 months.

Examples of the causes of difficulty are: believing that you (the trainee) know how to cure psychological problems; expecting partners to change because you are changing; using the spouse to practise skills on; and changing interests. We think another likely cause, not found in this study, is partners who do not listen and empathise as well as fellow students do.

In Truell's study, relationships with family members were also affected, 'uncomfortably' for five of the six participants. One trainee's siblings, for example, were wary of him being a counsellor. Another found that relatives asked her what to do about other family members, and then got blamed when things went wrong. Three of the participants reduced their involvement with their relatives, two felt their family relationships had improved and one saw no change.

All the participants said friendships had changed because of their training, e.g. becoming more selective, finding new friends, establishing 'clearer boundaries' with old friends, being less concerned with *having* to please their friends. Some were also criticised as being arrogant, weird etc. for doing counsellor training. Colleagues at work and the general public were similarly hostile at times and interested and encouraging at other times.

A contrasting finding was reported by Mackenzie and Hamilton (2007). They asked nine groups of first-year Certificate students about their expectations of counsellor training and how they saw the outcomes. Nearly all reported either an improvement in relationships, which they attributed to better listening skills and greater patience and tolerance, or no change.

A complementary perspective was offered by Nacif (2004), writing as the partner of a trainee counsellor. She says her commitment to the training 'had to be as crucial and selfless as my husband's' and that their lives were 'completely transformed' (p. 40). An initial problem for her was that she was excluded from a large part of her partner's life. She didn't understand the need for confidentiality until later but, even so, thinks she would probably have felt untrusted anyway. Then there was all the coursework and resulting lack of time together, and perhaps most of all the change in her husband. The subheadings of her article (which may not have been the author's choice) are dramatic: 'Loss of trust', 'The coursework nightmare', 'Sleeping with a stranger'. At times, she felt 'almost as if I have lost him'.

It may help you to be aware that you are likely to change considerably during counsellor training and that the changes may cause tensions in your significant relationships. Our experience is that couples and families who acknowledge these tensions and are able to talk them through are more likely to be able to integrate change and grow together. Talking about the course, the skills, values and principles, and sharing your learning, your enthusiasm and your questions seems to help, as long as you don't overdo it. However, it is also the case that for some trainees, increased self-awareness and changes in attitude can lead to significant changes in their personal lives.

relationships with the other students

> ▷ angry, assertiveness, boundaries, complaints, distressed, journal, relationships with friends etc., stress, trust

Generally, relationships between students in counsellor training are warm and supportive. However, there is also tension and conflict and, although they are often a sign of a healthy group, they can be demoralising for individuals and sometimes for the group. Bullying and harassment can also occur and should be taken very seriously.

Berne's (1964) idea of 'games' can be a useful perspective on some interpersonal problems. He used it to describe interactions with an ulterior motive on the part of one or more of the people involved and the games are played with different degrees of intensity and pathology. For example, one of the games is called 'Ain't it awful': one person complains, inviting the other to join in. If the complaints are not well-founded and you do join in, the game escalates and you both become more angry or depressed (though also supported and confirmed, in a sense).

However, you can decline, either the first time it happens (but it's easy to be 'caught up') or a subsequent time. For example, to decline the invitation to play 'Ain't it awful', you can say something like 'It sounds as if you've decided it's hopeless' (cognitive empathy), 'You sound despairing' (emotional empathy), 'I see things differently' (assertive expression of opinion), or 'What might you do about it?' (challenge to be constructive).

Bullying and harassment are extreme and unhealthy forms of conflict but they too can be resolved constructively. Like domestic violence, they tend to start with relatively minor things, e.g. having your views ignored, being the recipient of unreasonable demands and offensive remarks. Most of us are capable of behaving in these ways especially when stressed or frustrated but it is their *persistent* use that is usually taken to define bullying (Cartwright and Cooper 2007).

Ways of tackling bullying include assertive skills, reducing stress, clear organisational policies and developing a more inclusive culture. A useful first step, as with any problem, may be to write about it – as outlined in the entry on the Journal. The action you decide on might be a change of attitude, to try one or more of the more assertive skills, or to talk to someone. If there is no resolution or not enough progress, then the sequence of procedures outlined in the entry on Complaints becomes appropriate.

relaxation

> ▷ exercise, exercises, imagery, mindfulness, sleep, writing (expressive)

Relaxation techniques need to be chosen well and practised diligently. They can be very effective (Payne 2000) but two potential problems with them are their variety and the possible side effects described well by Lazarus and Mayne (1990): '... dizziness, floating ... paradoxical increases in tension; rapid heart rate; feelings of physical and psychological vulnerability; depression; fear of losing control; depersonalisation; dissociation; ... headache, intrusive images and thoughts; anxiety; irritability; ... hallucinations; and panic' (p. 261).If such unpleasant effects begin to occur when practising a technique, Lazarus and Mayne recommend strategies such as switching to an alternative technique, e.g. from breathing deeply to pleasant imagery or vice versa; or mini-relaxation sessions, e.g. ten 2-minute sessions rather than one 20-minute one; or the much more sophisticated approach of matching client personality to techniques.

These recommendations are still based on clinical experience only. Indeed, Lazarus and Mayne (1990) and Rosenthal (1993) are two papers that we don't think have been improved on. Rosenthal (1993) is a lively analysis of, and practical guide to, a wide range of procedures for 'unwinding', e.g. progressive muscular relaxation, guided imagery, meditation physical exercise, reflexology, t'ai chi, Alexander technique and breathing. He distinguishes between relaxation methods (as listed above) and distraction strategies such as changing attitudes and philosophies, humour, play and pets.

research, ideas for

> ▷ critical thinking, self-awareness

You may be required to produce a research proposal or carry out a research project as part of your training. If so, the first step is identifying a topic in which you are sufficiently interested. Finding a question which you are motivated to explore will make the hard work of carrying out research much more rewarding.

Here are some questions that might help you begin to identify a topic:

▸ What aspect of your own counselling would you like to know more about from your clients' perspectives?

‣ What could you learn from other counsellors: about how they work, how they deal with particular client issues, how they use techniques; how they manage issues of difference with clients such as spiritual beliefs, values etc.; what ethical dilemmas they experience and how they manage them etc.?

‣ What questions do you have about how clients or counsellors experience the therapeutic relationship?

‣ What would you like to understand better about how particular skills, techniques or approaches are used by counsellors or are experienced by clients?

‣ What issues relating to the boundaries of the therapeutic relationship interest you?

‣ What questions do you have around the experience and use of supervision?

‣ What questions do you have about the attitude of particular groups to counselling: whether and how they use it; access issues, stigma etc.?

‣ What aspects of counselling might be amenable to some form of measurement?

You will probably be able to add some general questions of your own to this list, and hopefully some potential topics will begin to emerge. You may also find it useful to look at a sample of counselling journals to get a flavour of the kinds of topics that are being researched by others. The next step is to refine or focus your topic into a research question, and consider whether the question is researchable, i.e. will it be possible to design a study which will gather meaningful data related to your question and begin to answer it?

research design, some general aspects of

> ▷ reading as a skill

Decisions to make in designing a research study include:

1 *Research philosophy.* Are you approaching the research from the perspective that there is an objective answer to be found to your question, or are you more interested in exploring the subjective experience of the people who take part in your study? The former position can be referred to as *positivist* while the latter is *non-positivist* (see McLeod 2003b).

2 *Quantitative or qualitative methods, or both.* Do you want to work with data in the form of numbers, measurements, rating scales etc. (quantitative), or in the form of words: text, interviews, written accounts, questionnaires using open questions (qualitative)? It is also possible (but more complex) to use a 'mixed method' and gather both qualitative and quantitative data.

3 *Participants.* Who do you want to gather data from? From peers, colleagues, clients (yours or others'), other counsellors, supervisors, members of particular groups, or even yourself?

4 *How will you recruit participants?* Will you do it by approaching individuals you already know or can identify as potential participants; through

r

particular organisations or agencies asking for volunteers; via advertising on a noticeboard or in a local paper; via a website or internet forum etc.?

5 *How do you want to gather your data?* Will you do it by interview, questionnaire, observation, rating scales, written responses, narratives or freewriting, journal keeping etc.?

6 *How will you analyse your data?* A number of specific procedures for analysing data can be found in research methods textbooks.

Having thought about provisional answers to these questions, it will be time to read up on specific methodologies and the literature and begin to refine your approach. A useful introductory text is McLeod (2003b). In our experience, counselling trainees tend to opt for qualitative rather than quantitative methods (though some excellent quantitative projects have been carried out). Questionnaires and semi-structured interviews are popular ways of gathering data; and Grounded Theory Analysis and Interpretive Phenomenological Analysis are popular ways of analysing the data.

research papers, reading

▷ **critical thinking, evidence-based practice, reading as a skill**

The research literature has not traditionally been part of counsellor training, except perhaps in passing. With the rise of evidence-based practice, this is changing fast, and trainee counsellors need to be able to understand and evaluate original research articles and to reflect on their implications (if any) for practice. This means understanding the limitations and strengths of different kinds of evidence and techniques (e.g. anecdotes, case studies, randomised controlled trials). It can be a daunting task despite some excellent textbooks, e.g. Robson (2002), McLeod (2003b), Cooper (2008). The following guidelines, based on those sometimes sent to reviewers of articles and papers submitted to refereed journals, may help:

- Is the research question clearly stated? (Journal reviewers are also concerned with originality.)
- Is it of interest to you (for reviewers, to the journal's readers)?
- Does the literature review tell the 'story' leading up to the research question, i.e. put it in context?
- Are key terms clearly defined?
- Is what the researcher actually did to collect the data described in enough detail so that, if you wished, you could repeat the study?
- How well motivated were the participants likely to have been?
- Are the measures valid?
- Are the results/data interpreted cautiously? Have alternative explanations been discussed?
- Are any conclusions or recommendations justified by the data?

These are general questions. More specific variations will apply to qualitative versus quantitative research, e.g. questions about sample size, bias and response rate for some quantitative studies. Whether or not to persevere with a paper you don't understand is discussed in the entry on Reading.

role play versus talking about real problems (as a practice client)

▷ client

The issue here is whether the person taking the client role in skills training should work with an issue that is real and present in their lives, or take on the role of an imaginary client with an imaginary issue. Generally we are in favour of the former, as it enables the work to be real, and the empathy and acceptance from the counsellor genuine.

A number of problems can occur with role play. The quality of the learning opportunity for the counsellor is highly dependent on the acting and improvisational ability of the person in the client role. Both parties know that the situation is false and can easily fall out of role. The counsellor is trying to empathise with feelings which are (probably) being portrayed rather than actually experienced, and as the session progresses, the person in the client role generally has to invent more and more details of the client's life in order to keep the session going. Whilst it is possible to use such scenarios to practise the mechanics of the core skills, we believe that the false context limits the value of the practice significantly.

Two arguments can be presented for using role play. Firstly, it can be argued that role play has the potential to allow trainees to experience working with some specific issues which are difficult and challenging, but unlikely to be brought to skills training by fellow students, e.g. mental health problems, sexual abuse or other serious trauma. This argument has some merit, but to portray such a client in a sufficiently realistic way as to provide meaningful practice is probably too much to expect of most students in counsellor training. Some courses have experimented successfully with hiring professional actors to take part in role play sessions and portray specific issues. The actors are able to prepare their roles in advance and are experienced in the kind of improvisation needed to make it feel real for the person in the counsellor role.

The second argument tends to come from students who find it difficult to identify issues in their lives that they feel able to work with, or have sufficient depth. This tends to be an issue only early in a training course. As trust within the group develops, trainees feel more able to risk bringing more sensitive issues, and with experience in the client role it becomes easier to identify issues which will work well and give the counsellor opportunities to practise the skills they are working on.

room, counselling

▷ **non-verbal communication, placement (finding)**

In selecting a placement, the room in which you will see clients is an important factor. A suitable room for counselling needs to be private. This includes not being able to be observed, and being sufficiently soundproof to avoid the possibility of conversations being overheard. It should also be in a location such that a client's confidentiality is preserved on entering and leaving the room, and there should be adequate arrangements for reception including a discreet waiting area.

You also need to be sure that you won't be disturbed for the duration of a session, and a DO NOT DISTURB sign is usually a wise precaution. Phones should be turned off or redirected. Chairs should be comfortable and equal in height (and perhaps ideally the same). Decor should be calm and relatively unobtrusive, and while some pictures or objects can help to create a therapeutic ambience, care should be taken to avoid anything which might have a particular meaning or association for a client. To be sure of this you will need to consider the diversity of clients you're likely to see. There will need to be a clock to enable you to keep time and that should ideally be visible to both you and your clients. If there is a pleasant view out of the window, you may choose to arrange the chairs so that your clients can see it.

Although it should rarely be an issue, security considerations may also influence how the room is arranged, depending on the client group. Some counsellors choose to sit nearer to the door if they consider that there is a sufficient risk from their clients, although some clients also prefer to sit near the door – especially initially, if they are anxious and unsure about trusting the counsellor. In any case, you should be comfortable that you will be able to summon help should it be needed. This might involve a 'panic button' installed in the room, a personal alarm, or knowing that someone is within earshot.

A counselling room may also contain resources for working in creative ways: art material, a selection of stones or buttons, and large sheets of paper and pens for brainstorming, mind-mapping etc.

room, training

▷ **non-verbal communication, video/DVD labs**

You may be unhappy or ill at ease about your course but unsure why. The setting is one possibility and the following description may help you to be clearer. Compromises are often necessary, however!

The main training room for a counselling course should be big enough to accommodate the whole group sitting in a circle, and should also allow space for breaking up into smaller groups for discussions, group tasks etc. Chairs should be comfortable and there should be supports for taking notes. Depending on the learning and teaching methods employed, there may be a range of other equipment available such as overhead projectors, flipcharts, PowerPoint facilities, and DVD or video replay. There may also be other resources such as art materials if appropriate. The room should of course be at a comfortable temperature, well ventilated, and lit adequately. It should be free from external interruptions or intrusive noise. According to BACP criteria for accredited courses, you should have a stable base room, which is available for the duration of the taught period.

Courses may also have other rooms available for experiential work (usually a less formal space with comfortable chairs or floor cushions) and space for splitting into smaller groups for group supervision etc. There will also be confidential spaces for skills practice in threes or fours, usually with recording facilities.

r

S

safety

> ▷ placement, room (counselling)

selection interviews

> ▷ presentations, selection interviews (preparation for)

What kind of interview might you be invited to? There aren't any surveys of counselling courses' selection procedures, but we'd expect the most widely used interviews to be semi-structured or unstructured, and one to one or a small panel, as is true of UK organisations generally. This is despite the recommendations of most writers about selection methods (e.g. Cook and Cripps 2005) to use structured interviews.

If you're faced with a structured interview, you may find it helpful to know that it is in effect an oral questionnaire which the 'interviewer' reads out and does not depart from. The validity of structured interviews is higher than that of unstructured interviews and they're seen to be fair – everyone is asked the same questions – but they have a number of drawbacks. First, applicants like them less than semi- or unstructured interviews: they tend to find them impersonal, which is particularly inappropriate when selecting – and recruiting – for a counselling course. Second, the interviewers tend to get bored. Third, devising the (set) questions is expensive. Fourth, some applicants may discover from previous applicants what the questions are, thereby gaining an unfair advantage.

Structured interviews come in two main variations, focused respectively on what you've done in particular situations and on what you would do in particular situations. The situations are closely related to work and based on a job description. Questions of both types are asked in unstructured interviews too, but the general emphasis in these is on personality, motives, attitudes, reason, goals etc., and the interviewer may not know what they're going to ask next, or may even struggle to think of a question.

Semi-structured or unstructured interviews are popular for good reason, and current thinking about their value may be changing (e.g. Blackman 2002; Blackman and Funder 2002). Moreover, some *interviewers* make highly valid judgements (though perhaps specialising in certain characteristics or jobs rather than being all-round good judges). The problem is finding out which ones! The general strength of unstructured interviews is a more free-flowing tone.

Interviewees may therefore feel more relaxed and behave more authentically (or, from an adversarial conception of selection interviews, be more likely to be 'caught off-guard').

selection interviews, preparation for

▷ **assertiveness, brochures, non-verbal communication, presentations, relaxation, self-awareness**

Preparing for an interview may help you feel calmer and more confident. At the least, it's a good idea to read the course information carefully and to think of one or two questions about it. Another possibility is to read your application form from the point of view of an interviewer. What might they want to ask you? (A sophisticated ploy would be to actually plant likely topics as 'lures', but that's probably too clever.)

Interviewers for counselling courses are (we think) much more likely to be interested in your mind and manner than your clothes, so we suggest comfort and simplicity as the main criteria for deciding what to wear. If it's a panel interview, though, the atmosphere will tend to be more formal, and you should consider dressing more smartly. You will be judged on your appearance, but good interviewers will be able to put aside this and other biases and focus on you. On the other hand, appearance and first impressions do have *some* relevance to being a counsellor: they can make forming a relationship with clients easier or harder.

Some interviewers have favourite questions but you'd need a reliable source to know what they are, and there are no standard ones. There are two main approaches, which can be called gentle probing and 'torpedoing'. The gentle probing approach is to ask you about things you're familiar with and press you for detail in an attempt to achieve authenticity. The torpedoing or stress approach is to try for the same goal but using surprise, e.g. the interviewer would ask at the start (from numerous possible questions, of course) a question like 'Are you smart or stupid?' presumably accompanied by a steely gaze. An interviewer on a training course run by one of us saw such questions as giving the interviewer the upper hand; he clearly saw interviews as battles, whereas we prefer a warmer, collaborative approach and don't recommend torpedoes. However, it's worth knowing that they may be launched.

We also recommend preparing some general topics like favourite books/authors (and why), influential people (and why), what makes you particularly angry, happy and sad and so on. There are books suggesting model answers to interviewers' questions but we suggest ignoring them. If you must, try Hodgson (2008), even though her subtitle implies an adversarial approach.

Far better, in our view, is to prepare by reflecting about relevant aspects of yourself and your experiences and then trust yourself to find words in the

S

interview. Another general strategy seems to us to be helpful here, apart from the obvious one of being reasonably calm and alert. It is to listen to the interviewer, both to her questions and to the way she responds to your answer. This means asking (to yourself) 'So what?' of a question, i.e. going beneath its surface to consider the purpose behind it. Ideally you then answer taking that purpose into account: your answer is relevant and helpful. Observe your interviewer's reactions to help you know when to stop talking. A skilled interviewer may say when she's heard enough ('Can I stop you there?') but your interviewer may not have this skill or may not wish to use it.

Two related practical bits of advice are that it's OK to ask for clarification ('Do you mean …?', 'I'm not sure what you mean by …', 'Do you want me to say more?') but perhaps twice at the most; and that it's also OK to refer to a (fairly brief) written list of your questions. And that seems to us to be plenty of advice on preparing for an interview; more seems likely to be inhibiting or to produce a mechanical, over-rehearsed, robot-like performance rather than true social contact.

selection procedures for counsellor training

▷ **age, choosing a counselling orientation, experience, good counsellors, motives, qualifications, readiness to begin training, self-awareness, strengths**

The standard approach to selection recommended in occupational psychology is broadly thus: describe the job; describe the qualities, experience etc. needed to do the job well; attract sufficient good applicants; assess the applicants. At each stage there are decisions to make and numerous research findings available to inform those decisions.

However, in practice, most selection procedures are less rigorous and more haphazard than this approach. There are also complicating factors: some general, e.g. that jobs change and that some jobs can be done well in very different ways; and some more specific to counselling, e.g. that there is no decisive evidence (though many opinions) on the qualities of the 'good counsellor' or on how much and in what respects trainees can and cannot realistically change as a result of being on a course.

An underlying tension for selection (directly relevant to this entry) is how open to be about the procedures. On the one hand, many trainees and counsellors value openness and a collaborative approach to counselling itself, and see selection in the same way. Moreover, applicants who feel trusting are probably more likely to relax and do themselves justice. On the other hand, people are generally adept at concealing negative aspects of themselves and pretending to have positive ones, and openness about selection methods may – probably will – aid such faking. From this perspective, selection is a battle of wits, a game of chess, rather than a collaborative relationship.

Our experience is that most applicants don't fake (or at least only a little, and more by omission) but that occasionally someone applies who in our view is not suited to counselling and would cause problems in the group. We don't want to help them be a more attractive and convincing applicant by being too open about selection methods!

A request from a potential applicant illustrates some of the tension between the two positions. She asked, 'Is there a word limit for the answer to the question on the application form asking for further information?' The tutor replied, 'No, but we like conciseness.' He was trying to be both helpful to her and fair to other applicants. It would give the inquirer an unfair advantage to coach her further (even this comment may have done so) but at the same time to have just said 'No limit' seemed too terse, too pure an example of the 'battle of wits' approach.

What qualities apart from conciseness might selectors be looking for? Well, even though ideas about effective counsellors vary and sometimes clash, some qualities are likely to be prominent: empathy, warmth and genuineness, the ability to reflect on and make constructive use of life experiences, the ability to listen, and tolerance for ambiguity.

You might at this point like to reflect on two questions that follow from this brief list:

1 What other qualities (assuming you agree with the list) do you see as important?
2 How would you try to measure them?

On the first question, some other possibilities are maturity, emotional stability, and critical thinking . If you're feeling discouraged at this point, please note that such lists are ideals; real applicants have patterns of strengths and weaknesses.

A further complication is that selection may look for different qualities depending on the orientation of the course, and there is some evidence that personality influences choice of orientation (e.g. Dodd and Bayne 2006). However, we think this should be a minor factor for selectors to bear in mind, except perhaps for very 'pure' orientations. For some models, and perhaps generally, *diversity* of background and personality is desirable, partly because the course group will then itself be more educational.

On the second question, of how best to try to measure the desired qualities, there is again a wide range of options, little agreement on which are best and no strong evidence to inform decisions. In practice, most courses probably use application forms and interviews and, in our view, depending on the number and quality of applicants, this may well be enough. However, another option is more like an assessment centre (sometimes called a development centre) with a variety of assessment techniques, such as case studies, questionnaires and role plays.

self-awareness

> ▷ assertiveness, co-counselling, interpersonal process recall, journal, lifeline exercise, motives, personal therapy, personality theory, psychological type, strengths, video/DVD labs

Ideas about the nature of 'self' vary widely. The influence of culture, whether we each have multiple selves or a single real self, the content of self, and how similar to self related terms like 'identity' and 'ego' are, and other issues are discussed with reference to personality theory by Funder (2007), to counselling by McLeod (2003a) and to aging and death by Brown (2008). McAdams' model, outlined in the entry on personality theory, may resolve some of the issues.

Many counselling skills and qualities depend on self-awareness. For example, empathy is aided by separating your own emotions from your client's emotions, and accurate awareness of aspects of yourself (both inward aspects and actions) is central to effective use of assertiveness skills, to managing stress and to identifying strengths. In this entry, we distinguish between three aspects of self-awareness: fluid inner self-awareness, relatively stable inner self-awareness, and outer self-awareness (Bayne et al. 2008), and suggest some ways of developing self-awareness in each sense.

Fluid inner self-awareness

Inner self-awareness in its fluid sense is awareness of one's thoughts, feelings, emotions, sensations, needs, wishes etc. This meaning is central to Self theories of personality. For example, Jourard defined the 'real self' as 'the real nature of a person's feelings, wishes and thoughts' (1964: 156) and as 'the ongoing flow of … spontaneous inner experience' (1971: 35). Rogers (e.g. 1961) defined 'self' in a similar way in his concepts of 'actualization of the real self' and 'congruence'.

Theorists differ in how aware of their 'real selves' they think most people are, how aware we can become, and the most effective ways of increasing such awareness. The main arguments for counselling trainees increasing their fluid inner self-awareness are that:

- the core counselling quality of genuineness is based on it, by definition;
- the core quality of empathy involves separating your emotions, reactions etc. from the other person's;
- the counsellor is correspondingly more likely not to be too upset or shocked by what clients tell them, and to listen well and to stay sufficiently composed.

Inner fluid self-awareness can be increased in many ways, e.g. Interpersonal Process Recall, experiential exercises, expressive writing and personal therapy.

Stable inner self-awareness

Stable inner self-awareness refers to patterns and tendencies within fluid inner self-awareness such as likes, dislikes, values, abilities and personality. Theorists differ on how much emphasis they place on individual differences in fluid versus stable elements of self. For example, Rogers and Jourard seem to suggest that there are no such elements, while for Jung and Maslow there are such tendencies as extraversion and introversion in real selves.

Stable inner self-awareness is relevant to counsellors for several reasons, discussed in the entries on personality and psychological type. It can be increased by looking for patterns in the fluid self, by accurate feedback from others (though your response to inaccurate feedback can also be useful) and by valid personality and other test results. The search probably doesn't end because the elements are only relatively stable: they develop, and they also become more or less relevant in different circumstances.

Outer self-awareness

Outer self-awareness is awareness of our behaviour and appearance and their impact on others. This too matters in counselling because of its potential effect on rapport and trust. It can be developed through feedback from others and watching yourself on video or DVD.

self-care

> assertiveness, boundaries, exercise, journal, relaxation, sleep, stress, time management

self-development

> experiential groups, journal, open circle, personal development, personal therapy, self-awareness, strengths, stress

self-esteem

> assertiveness, assessment (issues), feedback (receiving), good counsellors, rejection, self-awareness, strengths, stress

If you are prone to low self-esteem, you will need to consider ways of managing this during the challenges of your counselling training. Potential difficulties can arise in a number of ways.

Receiving feedback on your skills practice can be stressful, and some students have a tendency to be overly self-critical, not recognising what they have done well in a practice session. There is also a danger, when you listen to feedback from peers and tutors, that you only really hear the (hopefully constructive) criticisms, and do not give equal attention or weight to the positive feedback you receive. You can try to counter this tendency by making careful notes of the feedback you get, and disciplining yourself to note the positives first and in as much detail as the areas for development. If practice sessions are being recorded, then also record the feedback so that you can review it afterwards and make an accurate record rather than relying on your impressions.

Using the term 'areas for development' rather than 'weaknesses' may help; work towards seeing skills practice as an opportunity for learning and experimentation (i.e. try to suppress any perfectionist tendencies). Some groups find that the maxim 'there are no such things as mistakes, only learning opportunities' helps create a positive atmosphere and lessens the threat to self-esteem. Others find it corny!

The phenomenon of 'de-skilling' is a common experience during training. You will have started your course with some skills already in place, as a result of previous training or life experience, but many find that when they begin to focus consciously on using skills which were previously more instinctive or automatic, they go through a period where their skills become awkward: they feel clumsy, and as though they are not able to perform as well as before. It may help to recognise that this is a common experience, and to talk to the other students about it.

It may also be that you are now better able to critique your skills, and so are setting higher standards for yourself – you may be recognising that what seemed adequate before was less good than you thought. This has been described as a move from 'unconscious incompetence' to 'conscious incompetence' and you may be relieved to know that the subsequent stages are 'conscious competence' and 'unconscious competence'. If you have learned to drive you may find the analogy helpful: you probably initially struggled to change gears, then became able to do it smoothly whilst thinking about it, then eventually began to do it automatically.

If you have negative experiences of school, then returning to education, being in a class, having to write essays, and submitting them for marking may also raise issues relating to self-esteem. It may help to take some time to write a list of ways in which the present situation is different from when you were at school, and how you are different now. This may also be an issue you could choose to work with in skills practice, in personal therapy or through expressive writing.

When you begin to see clients, inevitably some clients will come for one or a few sessions and then stop turning up. It is important to recognise that this is a common occurrence in counselling, and is more likely to be as a result of issues in the client's life than a judgement on your competence or ability to help. Also inevitably, you will not be able to form effective therapeutic relationships with every client you see. The factors involved in finding a good 'fit' between client and counsellor are complex, and sometimes personality clashes, differences in social or cultural background or values, or indeed preconceptions or prejudices on the part of the client can mean that they do not feel comfortable with you as their counsellor.

It is important to avoid taking this personally and as a judgement on your competence as a counsellor. Issues such as these are best discussed in supervision, where hopefully you will be able to explore them and develop a balanced perspective.

In terms of self-esteem, two important principles are:

‣ Move away from making 'global' judgements about yourself, i.e. try to avoid drawing conclusions about yourself as a whole on the basis of one aspect you are not happy with (for example: 'I've never had a long-term relationship so I must be a terrible person'). To combat this, it helps to break things down to specifics, and recognise that you, like everyone else, are multifaceted. You might try listing those aspects of yourself that you are happy with and things that you do well, to contrast with those you do not.

‣ Avoid overvaluing particular pieces of evidence, and rushing to judgement about yourself as a result (for example: 'This client didn't find me helpful so I must be a terrible counsellor'; 'I didn't get a very good mark for this essay so I must be stupid'). Here you need to challenge yourself to look at a broader picture: for example, which clients have found you helpful? What other evidence is there about your worth as a counsellor?

Rogers (1961) saw self-esteem as strongly related to the levels of unconditional positive regard experienced from others, and applied to yourself. You may need to work on applying the conditions of empathy and acceptance to yourself as well to others. When self-esteem is vulnerable it can help to identify those friends, family etc. who do show you unconditional acceptance and regard, and try to spend time with them.

sexual attraction

> ▷ assertiveness, boundaries, decisions, ethics, relationships

Different considerations apply to sexual attraction between counsellor (including trainees), clients, tutors and colleagues, so we'll take each separately. Two general points seem worth making, though. First, feeling sexually attracted to someone is not a matter of shame or regret. Second, the difference between feeling attracted and behaving sexually is crucial, just as it is between feeling vengeful or murderous and actually hurting or killing someone.

Counsellor and client

It is always unethical for counsellors to be sexual with their clients. This is because of the power difference, however much you try to reduce that power (as we believe you should), because the research is clear that the result is damaging to clients (e.g. Russell 1993, 1996) and because of the effects on potential future clients and on the reputation of counselling. Clients need to be able to trust their counsellor.

If a client says they're attracted to you, we therefore suggest a gentle but firm 'No', an explanation of the kind given above, and listening empathically to their reaction. If this goes well – if your client feels respected and understood – it can be a turning point in the therapy.

If you feel sexually attracted to a client, we suggest discussing it in supervision and hope you will feel sufficiently trusting to do so. If not, then talk to a trusted colleague or counsellor.

Counsellors and ex-clients

This is much more arguable, and factors like length of the counselling relationship, your counselling orientation and respect for autonomy are relevant (Russell 1993; Bond 2009).

Trainee and tutors

As with ex-clients, views differ. Some organisations ban sexual relationships (or behaviour) between students and tutors; others require disclosure and that the tutor doesn't assess the trainee's work; others have no, or vague, policies. We suggest open discussion with the course group, reducing as far as possible uncomfortable and ambiguous situations for the student him- or herself, the group and the tutor. The main problems are that the student may feel isolated from, or at least different from, the others and that the group may lose some cohesion. However, these problems are not inevitable or intractable.

sexual orientation

> ▷ diversity, multiculturalism, self-awareness

Clients may bring sexual orientation as their presenting issue to counselling, or it may emerge as a problem after you've been working with them for some time. In either case it's important to explore your responses carefully and to reflect on your ability to work with this issue in an empathic and accepting way. You are trying to allow for possible unconscious assumptions and unconscious (or even conscious) prejudices which could easily be communicated to the client, and impinge on the work you are able to do.

It may be difficult to genuinely understand the experience of someone struggling with their sexual orientation, fears around 'coming out' and the phenomenon of internalised homophobia, for example, if you have not shared similar experiences. Whilst a parallel argument could be made around any number of client problems, research indicates that clients with sexual orientation issues have felt particularly misunderstood, or become frustrated with having to explain so much about, for example, gay culture to counsellors who do not share their experiences (King et al. 2007).

As a result, approaches such as 'gay affirmative therapy' have been developed in an attempt to ensure that clients who wish to can work with a therapist who has some specialist training and experience and will support them unconditionally in exploring, making choices and working through their consequences (see for example Davis and Neal 1996). This is not to say that it is impossible for 'generic' counsellors to work with sexual orientation issues, but that it requires the counsellor to have addressed their own issues in this regard, and be genuinely able to work in an accepting and empathic way; and furthermore that clients should be aware they have a choice, and could be referred to a specialist agency.

skills training

> ▷ client, feedback, good counsellors, skills versus qualities, video/DVD labs

Skills training is an important aspect of all counsellor training, and courses cannot achieve BACP accreditation without including systematic skills training as a major strand of the curriculum. Skills training is normally carried out in small groups, and is based around short practice sessions where one member takes the role of counsellor, another of client, and the remaining member or members keep time, take feedback notes on the skills demonstrated, and facilitate the process of debriefing after the practice session. There may be a tutor present some or all of the time to offer additional feedback. Roles are then rotated so that each member of the group takes a turn in each role. This offers a range of learning opportunities: to practise specific skills and receive feedback from both the client and an observer; to experience being in the client role and raise awareness of the impact the skills have; and to observe and evaluate the practice of others and learn from their strengths and areas for development.

Skills training groups are sometimes referred to as 'triads' (if they consist of three members or roles) or the activity may be referred to as 'video or DVD labs' if the practice sessions are recorded. Recording adds extra opportunities for watching and evaluating your performance, and considering the feedback you were given. It also gives you the chance to build up a record of your development during the course, and see directly the progress you have made at various stages.

Some guidelines for making good use of skills training sessions are:

Counsellor: You are the main focus of the session. Try to prepare by thinking about what it is you want to practise – this might be particular skills, a specific technique or approach, demonstration of key qualities such as empathy or congruence, or some aspect of session management like beginning, ending, time boundaries etc. Try not to opt for 'I'll just see how it goes …'. After the session, be prepared to give yourself feedback on what you did well, and what you might have done differently.

S

Client: Your role is to enable the counsellor to practise. While there may also be some therapeutic benefit for you as the client, this is not the main purpose of the session. Try to select material to talk about which is real, meaningful but not too 'heavyweight' and which will give the counsellor an opportunity to practise what it is that they want to. Be prepared to give the counsellor feedback on what you found helpful, what you found less helpful, the impact of particular interventions or approaches etc.

Observer(s): Your role is to give feedback to the *counsellor* (not the client). Avoid the temptation to become drawn in to the client's story/content. Focus on what the counsellor is doing and the impact it is having. Be prepared to give the counsellor feedback on what you think they did that was effective, what might have been less effective, and any alternative approaches or interventions which you think of that might be helpful to them. (When there is more than one observer, it is probably best if one person takes primary responsibility for feedback, others adding only any extra points they wish to make.)

Remember that feedback is someone else's perspective; it is not necessarily right or wrong – you must decide how useful any particular item of feedback is to you. We suggest that feedback is kept relatively brief and focused and is delivered in the order: (1) counsellor, (2) client, (3) observer(s).

There may be times when as a group you wish to review and discuss a recording made in the session but we don't think that doing this as a matter of course is the best use of the available time. It is better to use the time for practice and feedback, and the counsellor can review the recording at home.

skills versus qualities

> ▷ good counsellors, skills training

There has in the past been some dispute within the counselling profession about whether training should focus on developing skills or developing qualities. The argument for qualities comes mainly from the person-centred tradition. One view is that practising specific skills intended to demonstrate the qualities of empathy, unconditional positive regard and congruence in some way detracts from their meaning as qualities. In effect, by practising skills one could learn to 'appear' empathic, accepting and genuine, without actually being so. Moreover, if you focus on developing and living the core conditions, then you will come to embody them and they will inevitably be communicated to the client as part of your way of being.

A number of researchers in the 1950s and 1960s (e.g. Carkhuff and Truax 1967) were able to identify specific categories of interventions (or skills) which were used frequently by counsellors, and which could be seen to have a particular impact. It followed logically from this that counsellors could be trained to develop these particular skills, and might be more effective as a result. The converse of the arguments above applies here: however much you might *feel* empathy for the client, and *be* non-judgemental and genuine, these qualities are unlikely to be beneficial unless they are perceived by the client. By learning the skills which can be used to communicate these qualities, counsellors can make them more available to clients.

As with many such polarised debates, there is some evidence of a rapprochement towards a compromise position, where the importance of both skills and qualities is acknowledged. Egan (2007), for example, identifies the need for trainees to develop the *values* of pragmatism, competence, respect, genuineness, and client autonomy alongside the skills of attending, listening, empathy, probing and challenging. In examining empathy in particular, he sees it as having the characteristics of both a quality and a skill, in that it involves the willingness to allow yourself to be open to your client's feelings, and to work through on a cognitive level what they seem to be experiencing, alongside the ability to communicate that understanding so that the client can explore and clarify their own understanding.

sleep

▷ imagery, relaxation

Poor sleep is a serious threat to our well-being. We die without sleep, and lack of sleep, or poor quality sleep, contributes to accidents, poor decision making, putting on weight, anxiety and susceptibility to illness (Martin 2002; Horne 2006). It is not just an inconvenience, and sleeping well deserves a high priority.

You may therefore, if practical, investigate your current need for hours of sleep by going to bed at a regular time, not using an alarm for, say, a week and checking that you feel reasonably alert most of the time when you're awake.

Martin (2002) suggests a longer and more careful variation of this procedure:

1 Allow 2 weeks of freedom to wake up when you like.
2 Go to bed at about the same time each night. Note the time and estimate when you go to sleep.
3 Sleep as long as you need and note the time you wake up.
4 Calculate how long you slept.
5 Discard the figures for the first few days. (Martin argues that people in Western society tend to be sleep deprived so the first few days you may be catching up.)
6 The average time you sleep over the last few days is the amount you need (for most people, between 7 and 9 hours).

S

Improving your sleep is, like coping with stress, a matter of experimenting until you find a strategy that works for you. It may also be worth checking on any assumptions, e.g. if you believe you need 8 hours' sleep a night but 'only' have 6 or 7, you may be worrying unnecessarily: people vary widely in how much sleep they need, and may vary at different ages too.

It is also worth checking with a doctor if you have persistent problems with sleeping. About 10 per cent of the general population have one or more of the 80 or so sleep disorders and there are some effective treatments for them (Schenck 2007).

Some often-recommended strategies for sleeping better are:
- having a regular time for going to bed and waking up (same for weekends and week days)
- making your bedroom more peaceful
- putting a few drops of lavender oil on your pillow
- avoiding caffeine, nicotine, sugar, alcohol and fatty food in the evening
- eating a banana, oats or some nuts about an hour before going to bed
- taking catnaps
- taking exercise, but not close to when you go to bed
- having a change of mattress
- writing a list of things to do the next day
- using peaceful imagery and other relaxation exercises in bed
- taking a hot bath

Overall: if you have trouble sleeping, try to work out what's stopping you by reading, consulting others and observing yourself; discover your best sleep patterns and circumstances – and try to implement them.

staff

▷ brochures, tutorials

strengths

▷ application forms, feedback, good counsellors, psychological type, selection procedures, self-awareness

The concept of strengths has recently been revived and refreshed (e.g. Seligman 2002; Linley 2008), and it has implications for several aspects of counsellor training, including selection, self-awareness and overall philosophy and tone. Its revival has also brought a new clarity of definition and application to concepts like genuineness, authenticity and self-actualisation.

Linley's carefully expressed definition of a strength is 'a pre-existing capacity for a particular way of behaving, thinking, or feeling that is authentic and energising to the user, and enables optimal functioning, development and performance' (2008: 9). He discusses each phrase in his definition (pp. 10–13), some key points being:

- our strengths are inside us, either at birth or developed as children;
- when we use our strengths, we feel more real, fulfilled and energised;
- 'we learn better in the areas where we are already strong' (p. 13);
- doing something well isn't the same as enjoying it, though there is some overlap.

Many questions are raised: 'So we can't be anything we want to be?', 'Some strengths are genetic and some learned?', 'How can I discover what my strengths are?' and, more subtly, 'Is it possible to overuse a strength?' and 'Is it true – it's such a romantic idea – that our strengths, or some of them, can be hidden from us?'

A criticism of the approach and philosophy of emphasising strengths is that it can be seen as ignoring weaknesses – but this is too extreme. Linley puts the balanced position well: 'one should focus on using strengths *as much or as little as the situation requires*, while still *managing weaknesses* to the extent that they cannot be made *irrelevant* ...' (2008: 70, his italics). His position may, though, overemphasise the role of the situation.

Strengths develop through practice, but the practice is by definition enjoyable and fulfilling (you can be very good at something but if you don't enjoy it, it's not a strength). Chance also plays a part, e.g. a new context or a passing comment. A strength like curiosity, for example, can be enjoyed by detectives, scientists, journalists and in many other jobs and activities.

Buckingham and Clifton (2001) argued that the difference between acceptable performance and excellence is very slight. For example, 'In golf the top players average twenty-seven putts per round. The middling players average thirty-two. Similarly, the difference between the exemplary mentor and the run of the mill boss might simply be a few more questions asked and a few more moments spent listening. No matter what your profession, the secret to consistent near perfect performance lies in these kinds of subtle refinements' (p. 132). They then propose that achieving these refinements requires expertise, and that achieving this expertise for just five strengths 'is the work of a lifetime' (p. 133).

Identifying strengths

The question 'What are your strengths?' seems simple. Indeed, you may like to pause and answer it now. Linley suggests two problems in answering it well: that we're not used to talking about our strengths and that we don't have the words. He also thinks that there are 'likely to be hundreds of different strengths, and the majority have yet to be explicitly identified, defined or named' (2008: 16).

Linley (2008) and others are working on identifying strengths (over 100 by 2008). They find that when someone has a strength and it is reflected back to them, they feel understood and valued. An example of such a strength is *Lift* – improving the mood of others through being optimistic and encouraging. Another is *Bounceback* – using setbacks to achieve more than you expected. Other terms for strengths are more familiar – e.g. Curiosity, Kindness, Humility – though not always seen as strengths.

If your reaction to Lift, Bounceback etc. is to feel inadequate or despairing, that is *not* the intended effect of a strengths-based approach! Rather, the idea is for you to feel encouraged to look for your own strengths.

The orthodox approach to identifying your strengths, and often a good starting point, is to complete a questionnaire. Free questionnaires, scoring and interpretation are available at www.viastrengths.org and www.authentichappiness. org. New developments will be reported on the Centre for Applied Positive Psychology website, www.cappeu.org. An obvious limitation, though, is the point made earlier: there may be many strengths yet to be named.

Other strategies are to:

‣ notice what you really look forward to doing;
‣ notice what 'comes easily' to you, with the proviso that some people take one or more of their strengths for granted;
‣ notice what you miss doing (cf. Linley 2008: 75);
‣ take part in an Individual Strengths Assessment (ISA), developed at CAPP, which ideally needs a specialist interviewer or coach. The underlying method accepts that asking someone or oneself directly 'What are your strengths?' is too abstract; rather, questions like 'Tell me about a really good day for you', 'When do you feel most alive?' and 'What sorts of activities give you the most energy?' are asked as part of a conversation. The replies are carefully observed for clues, and the clues noted for later feedback. They may also be followed up at the time, looking of course for further evidence for or against a real strength. A supplementary and minor strategy in the ISA is to ask about activities that are weaknesses or draining;
‣ explore your memories of early childhood and ask others about you then: what themes and patterns can you identify and how are they related to your current experience and behaviour? Linley uses the concept of a 'golden seed' (e.g. 2008: 189) – when someone remarks on an ability or talent in us and we remember the remark. Teachers, relatives and guardians or parents are all likely sources (as they are of 'leaden seeds');
‣ explore who you admire and why (it may be easier to see some of your own strengths in someone else);
‣ ask other people who know you well when you're most energised and when you're at your best (see entry on Feedback);

- if you know your psychological type, read the descriptions for strengths that are characteristic of it and see if they apply to you.

There are further complicating factors in identifying strengths for some people and in some strengths. One is how developed or not the strength is. A second is that some strengths may be what can be called 'higher order': they are combinations of strengths which require *all* the constituent basic strengths to exist. A third is the role of context.

stress

> ▷ assertiveness, exercise, fears, loss, mindfulness, motives, rejection, relationships, relaxation, self-awareness, self-esteem, sleep, tutorials, writing (expressive)

The term 'stress' is usually used to mean feeling threatened and strained to an overwhelming degree, or close to it: there's too much to cope with. However, it is also used to mean too little going on, as in 'bored out of my mind', which implies that there's an optimum level of stress, and that 'challenge' or 'stimulation' might be better terms.

Counsellors and other helping professionals may be more likely than other occupational groups to deny that they are stressed. We may be better models of self-neglect than self-care. In particular, we may find it difficult to acknowledge when we need help, and then difficult to ask for it. Either way, we think that looking after yourself is a professional responsibility for counsellors and trainee counsellors and should be a priority in counsellor training.

Trainee counsellors obviously face all the normal (or at least quite common) potential sources of stress, like 'too much to do', travelling, fear of failure, doubts about one's own abilities, some relationships. But counselling brings others too, categorised as seven 'burdens' by Brady et al. (1995). The most stressful of these for many trainee (and experienced) counsellors is clients who are suicidal. Other particularly stressful 'client behaviours' include depression, aggression, lying, dependence and talking about abuse. Moreover, relatively minor rejections and losses, e.g. clients not arriving for a session or ending their counselling abruptly, can have a cumulative effect.

A second of the burdens is 'psychic isolation'. In the therapeutic relationship, the client's needs and interests come first, and – in many forms of counsel- ling – the counsellor's self-disclosure is limited or non-existent. However, sometimes counsellors and therapists behave in the same way in their personal relationships and may pay a high price, 'eventually losing a clear sense of self' (Brady et al. 1995: 13). Moreover, confidentiality may get in the way of seeking emotional support from friends, family and colleagues, who may in turn resent being shut out. As a further layer here, Henry et al. (1973, cited in Brady et al. 1995) reported that 60 per cent of psychotherapists in a survey said they had

S

few friends at school and felt 'somewhat isolated' there. The solution is obvious: counsellors, too, need close human contact and support.

A third burden is some other effects of therapeutic relationships. Brady et al. (1995) write that 'We alternate between sleepless nights fraught with recollections of hostility and anxiety incurred from characterologically impaired patients, and fleeting moments of realization that we have genuinely assisted a fellow human being' (pp. 15–16). We see this view as unhelpfully dramatic and think counsellors need realistic expectations about the limits of therapy and perhaps some clients who are untangling problems of life as well as those who are 'characterologically impaired'. Variety of clients in this sense is not always practical but we should try to make it practical.

Upsetting life events can reduce a counsellor's effectiveness at work and, conversely, being a therapist can disrupt personal life, e.g. partners and children feeling neglected. Storr (1990) referred to an exhaustion which leaves little emotional energy to spare. One effect of this on him was that he lost interest in reading novels. A particularly stressful aspect here is being calm and professional with clients who are talking about problems that are related to your own.

Each of us tends to react to too much or too little stress (or stimulation) in our own way, and the first step in coping is to know our individual signs. Early signs are particularly useful: the effects are less likely to become chronic, identifying the cause or causes is more feasible, less energy is wasted and less damage done. You may at this point like to reflect on your own reactions: how do *you* know when you're stressed? What are your early signs?

You might also ask people who know you well how *they* know when you're stressed. The lists below may help them and you:

Effects on thoughts and emotion
Difficulty concentrating
Anxiety, boredom, depression
Tired all the time

Effects on your body
Dry mouth
Frequent urination
Tics, and tension generally
Aches

Behaviour
Irritable
Accidents
Drugs
Problems with sleeping
Problems with eating

All of these signs, and others, may indicate illness or situational factors, so look for alternative explanations. That's stage 1 of a three-stage model of coping with stress, then: monitoring yourself from time to time for certain clues and patterns, but – to repeat – as a professional responsibility, not obsessively or narcissistically. Stage 2 is choosing a coping strategy, and stage 3, action, is trying out the strategy and evaluating how well – or whether – it works.

Some strategies are effective for most people, e.g. social support, expressive writing, relaxation, physical exercise, but within each of these strategies there is lots of flexibility and choice, and they themselves can cause further stress: confiding in one person may bring support and solace but increase or cause problems with another.

An assertive attitude to mistakes can be helpful here, e.g. accepting that much of the time things go wrong as a normal part of life and that everyone makes mistakes. Leary et al. (2007) and Neff and Vonk (2008) called a similar idea 'self-compassion'. It involves being kind to yourself when things go badly, seeing negative experiences (presumably up to a point) as normal, and 'mindful acceptance', i.e. being aware of feeling angry and upset (say) but not over-identifying with those feelings and associated thoughts.

Not much is known so far about matching personality to strategies for coping with stress, or indeed how useful this idea is (and the same is true of matching clients' personalities with therapists' or with approaches or techniques). Finding the best strategies is therefore a matter of experimenting on yourself, perhaps with the help of psychological type theory (e.g. Bayne 2004). The theory suggests that each of the following activities will be helpful either to different kinds of people or with different levels of stress in the same person:

- Join a group, phone someone.
- Write a journal, walk (alone), read, do nothing.
- Feed your senses, e.g. cook, paint, garden.
- Feed your mind, e.g. read about a theory, study something new, fantasise, design something.
- Analyse something, solve a puzzle.
- Do something caring, do something that involves decisions of like/dislike.
- Organise something, make a plan, make a list of things to do.
- Abandon a plan, play in an unstructured, free-flowing way.

We suggest that you choose part of one of these categories and make it more specific. What appeals to you? You may be drawn to apparently inconsistent possibilities. The theory can cope with this, and in any case what matters is what feels right to you.

Some of the most promising and empirically supported techniques for coping with stress are discussed in other sections of this book, e.g. physical exercise, relaxation, expressive writing. Norcross and Guy (2007) is a detailed review of coping with stress for therapists.

study skills

▷ brochures, critical thinking, essays and reports, notes (making), reading, strengths

Many books offer advice on how to study but in our view they tend to see one way as best or to give too few options. They ignore or underestimate individual differences.

For example, Weiten (2007) recommends setting up a schedule for studying, allocating definite times, and setting up one or two specific places to study in (pp. 26–7). This advice, though based on research, suits some people well and others not at all. It is too general, and for a substantial number of people it is too planned and too restrictive; they work best with a more spontaneous, flexible approach.

Therefore, we suggest that the best thing to do with advice on how to study – however authoritative the tone or source – is to think critically about it and to experiment until you find the best ways for you. Also, discuss with colleagues how they study: the idea here is to open up possibilities and perhaps feel more encouraged to experiment.

The same notion applies to 'learning styles'. Although the existence and value of learning styles is controversial, students and tutors do vary in their liking for different methods. For example, brainstorming is pointless and even threatening for some people but a pleasure for others. Similarly, you may have a strong preference for theory rather than 'workshops' or vice versa and it may therefore be worth checking on the teaching methods emphasised by a course you're considering applying to.

supervision, preparation for

▷ critical thinking, presentations, supervision (process), taping, trust

Preparing for supervision first involves identifying the issue or issues you will talk about. Take some time to reflect on your work with your current clients, and any who have recently ended. Identify areas where you are having difficulty; experiencing doubt or uncertainty about the way you are working; feeling challenged or inadequate; have concerns (perhaps about the client's issues, progress or welfare); or are feeling stuck or unsure what to do next. These are your potential issues for supervision. If most of your issues seem to be arising from a particular client then you may decide to present that client, and this is often seen as the norm for a supervision session. However, it is also possible to explore an issue which you may be experiencing in different ways with different clients, or indeed a more general concern about your counselling or your personal development.

When you are presenting a particular client, remember that the main purpose of supervision is not to discuss the client and their history, and speculate about what may be going on for them, although some of the time may be spent doing this and it may be useful. It is to examine the work you are doing with the client, to make sure that the client's needs are being met, and to explore ways in which you can be as effective as possible in your work. So in preparing to present a client you should prepare sufficient information about the client, their issues and their goals for the supervisor or group to be able to put your experience in context, but you should focus more on how you have been working with the client. This should include some information about the relationship you've developed, the skills and strategies you have been using and some evaluation of what you're doing well and what you could be doing better.

You may also wish to say something about the feelings you experience in working with this client, and any issues they raise for you. You can then describe the difficulties or challenges you are experiencing, identify what specific questions you'd like to address in supervision, and what you hope to get out of the session. You should avoid preparing so much material to present that you limit the time for exploration and discussion. If you're able to record sessions with your clients, an audio extract is a useful resource to bring to supervision as it gives a more rounded impression of the relationship and the way you're working.

supervision, process of

> ▷ assertiveness, boundaries, feedback, language, supervision (preparation), trust

At the most basic level, the process of supervision involves three stages:

1 An initial presentation, where the supervisee outlines the client work or issue they wish to explore and identifies what they want to get out of supervision.

2 A period of exploration, discussion and reflection, where the supervisor and supervisee or group examine the issues in more detail, explore different perspectives, and try to develop a better understanding of the issue, and possible ways forward.

3 A period of summarising and focusing, where the supervisee is encouraged to identify what they have learned from the session and what goals and strategies they have identified for future work.

Hawkins and Shohet (2006) identify seven modes of supervision which are useful guides to the kinds of work that can be done separately or in combinations during stage 2 above. These are:

- Reflect on what the client said and did, avoiding premature theorising.
- Explore the strategies and interventions used by the counsellor, and possible alternatives.

▸ Explore the counselling process and relationship.
▸ Focus on the counsellor's 'counter-transference'.
▸ Focus on the 'here-and-now' process (in supervision) as perhaps mirroring aspects of the counselling itself ('parallel process').
▸ Focus on the supervisor's or supervision group's 'counter-transference'.
▸ Focus on multicultural factors.

The summarising and focusing stage (stage 3) is important as it encourages the supervisee to pull together what is often a wide-ranging discussion or exploration, and identify what is most important and relevant for them. They are then in a position to consider what they will take forward from the session in a practical way by identifying goals for themselves and strategies for achieving them. These might include specific plans for working with the client under discussion or broader-focused goals and strategies for personal or professional development.

support

▷ **beginnings, trust**

t

taping counselling sessions

▷ assertiveness, boundaries, ethics, feedback, skills versus qualities

How do you feel about tape recording some of your counselling sessions? The obvious advantage of taping a counselling session is that you and your supervisor or supervision group can experience more directly and vividly what actually happened. The feedback may therefore be more useful. However, this advantage may have corresponding drawbacks: you or your client may feel inhibited or otherwise affected and the session may be less authentic. Moreover, tapes may encourage an undue focus on micro-skills and a neglect of the relationship and the core qualities of counselling.

Our experience is that the potential value of taping far outweighs the problems. You can listen to or view, sometimes repeatedly, nuances, non-verbal behaviour, tone, timing etc.: very rich material for reflection and feedback.

There are several practical issues. One is how exactly to ask your clients, and some careful preparation is probably advisable here. The relevant assertiveness skill is making a request, and you may find it helpful to develop some phrases and practise them as recommended in that entry. Ethically, your request should include enough information for informed consent. As in consent to be a research participant, it should also include the purpose of making the recording (e.g. so that you can work on your skills), information about who will see or listen to it, assurance that it will be kept securely, when it will be destroyed, and that your client can change their mind at any point during or after the session, i.e. withdraw their consent. That is their right and you fully accept it.

That may seem a formidable list but in practice many clients welcome the extra attention, especially if they feel their confidentiality will be respected. (In this respect, audio tapes are clearly more anonymous and confidential than videos or DVDs.)

A subtle aspect of asking clients if they will agree to being taped is that you may sabotage the request by conveying your own discomfort. You may therefore need to resolve your own anxieties first, for example through the journal method or talking to a tutor.

Another potential problem is that the agency you have a placement with doesn't allow recording. Feltham and Dryden (2006) suggest challenging this, and they point out that Carl Rogers was one of the pioneers of such recordings (p. 15). However, a diplomatic approach is probably best, and, as with asking clients, a response of 'No' should of course be respected.

Some clients probably say 'Yes' to a session being taped when they mean 'No' – they want to please or they feel in a subordinate position. We think you as the counsellor should listen sensitively for any doubts or anxieties but that your responsibility is to do this and to be clear in your request; it is not to make decisions for your client.

Who owns the content of the tape? What, for example, if your client owns the content and chooses to play the tape to others? The desirable ethical balance to find here is between over-concern on the one hand and respect for the well-being of everyone involved on the other. Finally, once you're ethically in possession of a tape of yourself counselling, there are decisions to be made about what to play to your supervisor or supervision group and what to ask for feedback on.

time management

▷ assertiveness, decisions, self-awareness, values

People often say 'There isn't enough time'. From an existential point of view this is absurd. There's as much time as there is, and it's up to us to choose priorities. Psychological type theory offers a more sympathetic, less steely perspective: that some people's approach to time is to *manage* it, while for others, time just happens, it *flows* (Bayne 2004). Both approaches can be effective but each is more likely to work best for you when (a) it suits you, (b) you trust yourself and are skilful in using it, and (c) others who are affected by your approach trust you to deliver on time, even when they strongly favour the opposite approach.

Traditional time management courses are biased towards one approach and against the other (the flow approach). They can therefore leave those who don't like to manage time defeated, demoralised, or struggling conscientiously with techniques that don't suit them. We suggest you experiment (either in thought or behaviour) with the following sets of techniques, to find if one or more of them works best for you:

Techniques with time
1 Timetable and calendars. Lists that are specific; tick off each item as you finish it. Work steadily and 'one step at a time'. Start early to avoid last-minute pressure.
2 Lists as overviews. Work in bursts and accept inactive periods as recovery/germination.
3 Work on whatever seems urgent at that moment. Find ways to make the work fun.
4 Have many projects at different stages, and rely on inspiration and the imminence of deadlines to move them forward.

transcripts

▷ critical thinking, language, non-verbal communication, skills training

A transcript is a written verbatim record of a session or an extract from a session made from an audio or video/DVD recording. It is a valuable tool for reflection, analysis and evaluation, in that you are able to review exactly what was said by both counsellor and client and understand how the interaction between them unfolded. Preparing a transcript can be a somewhat laborious task, but it can have great value in allowing you to see the detail of what was going on. You are likely to have to produce transcripts for assessments such as process reports, and perhaps presentations of recordings.

Some guidelines for preparing transcripts:

- Think carefully about how you are going to set out your transcript:
  - ▷ Allow plenty of space – wide margins and space between counsellor interventions and client responses. This makes it easier to read and may be useful for adding notes or comments later.
  - ▷ Distinguish between the counsellor's and the client's talk in a visible way, such as a different font or colour.
- Think about how best to use the technology available to you. The easiest way to transcribe is to use an audio device with a foot switch control for pause, rewind etc. If you are able to get hold of one of these it may be worth transferring the sound track from a video recording to audio to do most of the transcription, and add non-verbal communication later. Otherwise make sure you set yourself up comfortably and ergonomically with your replay device, remote control if used, headphones and paper/pen or computer, as you are likely to be there for a while. Increasingly, computer software packages for sound and video editing are available, which some might find helpful with this task.
- Write exactly what is said. People rarely express themselves verbally in coherent grammatical sentences but it is important to produce an accurate record of the words used. The precise way you or the client said something may turn out to be significant in terms of its meaning or its impact.
- Record as much non-verbal communication as you can. Transcripts should include 'ums' and 'aahs' etc. but you should also try to make a note of any significant changes in volume, intonation and so on; and, if transcribing a video or DVD recording, changes to posture, facial expression, gestures etc.
- Indicate pauses and any instances of the client and counsellor talking over or interrupting each other in your transcript.

Some courses may ask you to prepare an annotated transcript, which includes reflective, analytical or evaluative comments from you. This is most easily done by splitting your pages into columns, with the transcript down the left side, and space to add your comments in a right-hand column. This may look neater if presented in a landscape rather than a portrait format.

For a very detailed approach to transcribing conversations, you may like to have a look at the literature on conversation analysis from the discipline of linguistics (see for example Ten Have 2007). Conversation analysts have a range of conventions for recording tone, volume, intonation, inflexion, and pauses etc. which enable them to produce transcripts that are very rich in detail and information, and thus provide more material for analysis. Whilst this level of detail would not be realistic (for a 10–20 minute extract) or necessary in the context of a counsellor training course, it will give you a flavour of what can be done with transcripts as a research tool.

trust in the course group, developing

▷ **beginnings, open circle**

A training group is a safer and more productive place to be when trust has developed. Individuals vary in their ability and willingness to trust others, often on the basis of past experiences, so the development of trust is likely to be a gradual process. Your tutors are likely to include activities early on the course that are intended to facilitate this process. These will encourage sharing within the group, moving from an initially superficial level towards greater depth and intimacy. Provided that an ethos of empathy, genuineness and acceptance is also developing then such activities usually lead to greater trust, as members find that they can share aspects of themselves without being judged or exploited as a result.

You can contribute to this development by monitoring your own thoughts, feelings and experiences. Try to be aware of what you are choosing to say and what you are holding back. Reflect on why you might be doing so. Also be aware of your reactions to what others say – what do you feel, and what do you communicate to them? Are there particular people you're finding it difficult to trust, or experiencing negative reactions from or towards? Reflect on what might be behind this – for example, do they remind you of someone from your past? Consider how much of this you might be able to share with others or the group. Remember that it is possible to own your reactions to someone else and communicate them without that implying a judgement upon them. A useful principle to apply to sharing in a group is to challenge yourself to stretch – to go a bit beyond what is comfortable and easy for you – but not to stretch too far so that you find yourself stuck well outside your 'comfort zone'.

Some people may have particular issues with trust and may take a long time to find their way properly into the group, or they may test the group in some way, perhaps by revealing something quite risky, making negative statements about themselves, or behaving in difficult or confrontational ways. The principles of empathy, acceptance and genuineness apply here – if the response to such 'tests' is to demonstrate understanding, to avoid making judgements and show acceptance, and to own and express congruently your response, then it is likely that the person concerned will feel more able to trust as a result. Hopefully your tutors will model such responses and be able to facilitate the development of trust effectively.

There may be times as the course develops when particular issues occur which can have an impact on trust. These should be raised and discussed with tutors or at community meetings where they can be worked through by applying the principles above.

tutorials

▷ assertiveness, tutors

Tutorials may be voluntary or required. The tutor may have something they want to discuss with you but probably what is discussed will be up to you. If you don't have a particular problem or problems, you may want to 'touch base'. A more formal structure for some tutorials is:

1 You say what you'd like to discuss.
2 You agree an agenda.
3 You discuss, and try to clarify and resolve, any problems.

tutors and contact time

▷ assertiveness, fears, study skills, time management, tutorials

There is a tension in higher education between self-directed learning (the student as scholar) and having a 'fair share' of time with tutors (the student as customer or consumer). How available should tutors be? You may like to pause at this point and reflect on (a) your immediate response to this question and (b) your more considered response (which may be the same).

Two related tensions are about assessment and about how courses are 'sold'. Thus, tutors may feel pressured to pass students' work in order to keep the students on the course, and students may feel they have a right to pass (or pass well) because they have paid. Similarly, descriptions of courses and universities in brochures or on websites may be unrealistic because of competition for students.

Our view is that students are much more like scholars than customers. In practice, this means partly that tutors are as clear about assessment guidelines and marking criteria as they reasonably can be, and that we mark fairly, constructively and accurately. It also implies that students work fairly independently and generally try other ways of resolving problems before asking tutors for help.

t

Our experience is that most students ask for *less* contact time than the official allocation, and a few (say 1–3 out of 24) ask for considerably more. Both kinds of behaviour are ambiguous. Those who ask for little or no one-to-one contact are either very self-sufficient, or indifferent, or not assertive or too modest. We currently have an opt-in system of tutorials, and making this compulsory would be a way of counteracting the too-modest position. There might be a cost, though: how consistent with the spirit and ethics of counselling would this be?

Those students who ask for more (or a lot more!) contact time are either struggling for good reasons or are less confident. Very occasionally, they may be playing a game. One option – or requirement, really – for tutors is to challenge the low confidence or the game. There are examples of such challenges in the entry on relationships with other students. It is better for students to challenge themselves first, but good outcomes can happen either way.

An indication of what tutors (in universities) do apart from teaching on your course may help you decide about the amount of contact time you ask for. Most academics do most of the following as well as various kinds of teaching (Radford 2003):

- Research
- Scholarship (particularly trying to keep up to date with their specialisms)
- Professional practice
- Preparation for teaching
- Assessment
- Course development
- Selection
- Administration
- Committee work

Radford also points out that the demands are increasing because of larger numbers of students, and various internal and external assessments of research and teaching.

Here is a day in the life of one of us:

Forty-three emails and four phone messages first thing this morning. Most of the emails are from a closed discussion group. Others are from students about placements and essays; and from colleagues about teaching observations and other students, the post room closing early today, meetings, and so on – the ebb and flow, I imagine, of most organisations. I print some emails (the dream of a paperless office!), reply to a few and delete nearly all.

The morning is clear of teaching and meetings so I go to the library and check the details of some new books for a reading list, find a great paper in a current journal and talk to one of my students who is despairing about finding a book she wants for an essay. Back to two new phone messages and 15 new emails, and return the calls, both to potential applicants. Then discussions in the corridor and photocopy room with colleagues about, respectively, a chapter they're writing, football, an ethical issue, and another colleague's eccentric but endearing behaviour.

Collect photocopies for the afternoon's teaching. Check these over a sandwich. Then it's a tutorial with an enthusiastic student (20 minutes), my clinical supervision group (1½ hours), a workshop with 20 students (1 hour), and an unscheduled tutorial with a worried student (15 minutes). They go well (which of course is not always so) and I go home thinking about tomorrow: no teaching so it's one or more session of marking, reading a book proposal which I'm reviewing for a publisher (is a second edition a good idea?), writing and making notes for teaching, and/or other writing (many possibilities here: letters, manuscripts, chapters, papers). My way of working is to have piles for each 'task' on the floors of two rooms: I move the piles around from time to time, and something – an imminent deadline or a much less tangible factor X – leads me to do one of them.

And that's a fairly typical day for one university tutor. The main point, though, is to ask you to be assertive (see entry in this book) about your requests for contact time, and we will try to be assertive in return, and to balance being approachable with not being swamped.

t

u

upset, feeling

▷ distressed

V

values

▷ assertiveness, decisions, self-awareness, strengths

Your values describe what is most important and least important to you, and emotions are good clues to values. For example, if you groan whenever Manchester United are mentioned positively, this suggests a low value for that team or for football in general or for aspects of English premier league football. The 'whenever' is important: values are usually defined as enduring beliefs about what matters to you and what doesn't matter.

Most lists of values are abstract nouns, e.g. Love, Humility, Pleasure, Wealth, Expertise, Fame, but they need not be. For example, owning a particular house might be a (or the) top core value for someone who doesn't want to include it within Security, Escape from 'normal life', Environmental friendliness, Status etc. Generally, though, it is clearer to work through to greater abstractness.

Clarity about your values makes being assertive (e.g. saying 'no') and making decisions more straightforward. Helping clients clarify their values can be a useful counselling strategy. Therefore, counselling courses sometimes include a session on values. Patrick (2003), writing about her experience as a student with a values workshop, found 'several values, stumbling around ownerless' and some stimulating clashes between values she claimed as important to her and those she actually acted on.

There are numerous ways of exploring and identifying values (Simon et al. 1995) and it is usually – and logically – assumed that it is desirable for each person to focus on a few core values. This is because it is not possible to do everything well; our time and energy are limited.

A direct approach, in several steps, is first to ask yourself, 'What really matters to me?', and, perhaps separately, 'What really doesn't matter to me?', and to make two lists. Single words or brief phrases may be most useful.

The second step is to decide which values are your top and bottom priorities, aiming for five or so (say) in each set. This may not be a quick process and you may wish to refine your choices as your awareness deepens, or as you and your life change.

Six further options are to:

▸ Examine the origins of each value, as a way of checking its real importance to you.

- Look for possible inconsistencies between your values, and try to resolve them, change one or both of the conflicting values, or just accept the inconsistency.
- Look at consistencies between your values and your behaviour, as Patrick (2003) did.
- Focus on changing one or more of your values.
- Express the values as goals (specific steps).
- Relate your goals to your values, again with consistency and priorities in mind.

video/DVD labs

▷ skills training

visualisation

▷ imagery

W

work

▷ careers in counselling

writing, academic

▷ assessment, essays and reports

writing, expressive

▷ freewriting, journal

Writing freely about your experiences – usually troublesome ones but also those which are more positive – is an application of the ideas that (1) *not* expressing thoughts and feelings is stressful, (2) there is a human need to express them and (3) expressing them helps us clarify and put them in perspective. This latter idea is also, of course, consistent with counselling. The aims are to reduce confusion, clarify emotions, wishes, values and thoughts, and therefore free us better to act in the present. There is an extensive and thoughtful research literature supporting its general effectiveness (e.g. Wright 2005; Frattaroli 2006; Lyubomirsky et al. 2006).

References

Aamodt, M. G. (2001) Letters of recommendation. In S. G. Rogelberg (ed.), *Encyclopaedia of Industrial/Organizational Psychology*, 5th edn. Newbury Park, CA: Sage.

Aamodt, M. G. (2007) *Industrial/Organizational Psychology: An Applied Approach*, 5th edn. Pacific Grove, CA: Wadsworth Publishing.

Adams, K. (1990) *Journal to the Self: 22 Paths to Personal Growth*. New York: Warner Books.

Anderson, L. and Krathwohl, D. (2001) *A Taxonomy for Learning, Teaching, and Assessing: A Revision of Bloom's Taxonomy of Educational Objectives*. London: Merrill.

Arthur, R. A. (2001) Personality, epistemology and psychotherapists' choice of theoretical model: a review and analysis. *European Journal of Psychotherapy, Counselling and Health* 4, 45–64.

BACP (2009a) *Criteria for the Accreditation of Training Courses*. Lutterworth, Leicestershire: BACP.

BACP (2009b) *Ethical Framework for Good Practice in Counselling & Psychotherapy*. Lutterworth, Leicestershire: BACP.

Barker, C. (1985) Interpersonal process recall in clinical training and research. In F. N. Watts (ed.), *New Developments in Clinical Psychology*. Chichester: BPS Wiley.

Bayne, R. (2004) *Psychological Types at Work. An MBTI Perspective*. London: Thomson.

Bayne, R. (2005) *Ideas and Evidence. Critical Reflections on MBTI Theory and Practice*. Gainesville, FL: Center for Applications of Psychological Type.

Bayne, R. and Horton, I. (eds) (2003) *Applied Psychology. Current Issues and New Directions*. London: Sage.

Bayne, R., Jinks, G., Collard, P. and Horton, I. (2008) *The Counsellor's Handbook. A Practical A–Z Guide to Integrative Counselling and Psychotherapy*, 3rd edn. Cheltenham: Nelson Thornes.

Bayne, R. and Thompson, K. L. (2000) Counsellor response to clients' metaphors: an evaluation and refinement of Strong's model. *Counselling Psychology Quarterly* 13, 37–40.

Bensley, A. (2008) Can you learn to think more like a psychologist? *The Psychologist* 21, 128–9.

Berne, E. (1964) *Games People Play*. New York: Grove Press.

Blackman, M. C. (2002) Personality judgement and the utility of the unstructured employment interview. *Basics and Applied Social Psychology* 24, 240–9.

Blackman, M. C. and Funder, D. C. (2002) Effective interview practice for accurately assessing counterproductive traits. *International Journal of Selection and Assessment* 10, 109–16.

Boice, R. (1994) *How Writers Journey to Comfort and Fluency. A Psychological Adventure.* London: Praeger.

Bond, M. (1986) *Stress and Self-awareness. A Guide for Nurses.* London: Heinemann.

Bond, T. (2009) *Standards and Ethics for Counselling in Action,* 3rd edn. London: Sage.

Bradley, L. (2007) *The Rough Guide to Running.* London: Rough Guides Ltd.

Brady, J. L., Healy, F. C., Norcross, J. C. and Guy, J. D. (1995) Stress in counsellors: an integrative research review. In W. Dryden (ed.), *The Stresses of Counselling in Action.* London: Sage.

Brown, G. (2008) *The Living End. Death, Aging and Immortality.* Basingstoke: Palgrave Macmillan.

Bruna Seu, I. (2006) Feminist psychotherapy. In C. Feltham and I. Horton (eds), *The Sage Handbook of Counselling and Psychotherapy,* 2nd edn. London: Sage.

Buckingham, M. and Clifton, D. O. (2001) *Now, Discover your Strengths.* London: Simon and Schuster.

Carkhuff, R. and Truax, R. (1967) *Toward Effective Counselling and Psychotherapy.* New York: Aldine Publishing Company.

Cartwright, S. and Cooper, C. L. (2007) Hazards to health: the problem of workplace bullying. *The Psychologist* 20, 284–7.

Clarke, K. M. and Greenberg, L. S. (1986) Differential effects of the Gestalt two-chair intervention and problem-solving in resolving decisional conflict. *Journal of Counseling Psychology* 33, 11–15.

Cook, M. and Cripps, B. (2005) *Psychological Assessment in the Workplace. A Manager's Guide.* Chichester: Wiley.

Cooper, M. (2008) *Essential Research Findings in Counselling and Psychotherapy.* London: Sage.

Corey, G. (2005) *Theory and Practice of Counselling and Psychotherapy,* 7th edn. London: Thomson.

Corey, M. S. and Corey, G. (1998) *Becoming a Helper,* 3rd edn. London: Brooks/Cole.

Cottrell, S. (2008) *The Study Skills Handbook,* 3rd edn. Basingstoke: Palgrave Macmillan.

Crane, R. (2008) *Mindfulness Based Cognitive Therapy.* London: Routledge.

Daines, B., Gask, L. and Howe, A. (2007) *Medical and Psychiatric Issues for Counsellors,* 2nd edn. London: Sage.

Daniels, J. and Feltham, C. (2004) Reflective and therapeutic writing in counsellor training. In G. Bolton, S. Howlett, C. Lago and J. K. Wright (eds), *Writing Cures. An Introductory Handbook of Writing in Counselling and Psychotherapy*. London: Brunner-Routledge.

Davies, D. and Neal, C. (eds) (1996) *Pink Therapy. A Guide for Counsellors and Therapists Working with Lesbian, Gay and Bisexual Clients*. Buckingham: Open University Press.

Daw, B. and Joseph, S. (2007) Qualified therapists' experience of therapy. *Counselling and Psychotherapy Research* 7, 227–32.

Dexter, G. (1996) A critical review of the impact of counselling training courses on trainees. Unpublished PhD thesis, University of Durham.

Dickson, A. (1987) *A Woman in Your Own Right*, rev. edn. London: Quartet.

Dobson, P. (1989) Reference reports. In P. Herriot (ed.), *Assessment and Selection in Organizations*. Chichester: Wiley.

Dodd, N. and Bayne, R. (2006) Psychological types and preferred specific counselling models in experienced counsellors. *Journal of Psychological Type* 11, 98–113.

Doyle, C. E. (2003) *Work and Organisational Psychology. An Introduction with Attitude*. Hove: Psychology Press.

Dryden, W. (1991) A dialogue with Arnold Lazarus. *It Depends*. Milton Keynes: Open University Press.

Dryden, W. (1994) Possible future trends in counselling and counsellor training, *Counselling* (August), 194–7.

Dryden, W. and Feltham, C. (1994) *Developing Counsellor Training*. London: Sage.

Egan, G. (2007) *The Skilled Helper: A Problem Management and Opportunity Development Approach to Helping*, 8th edn. London: Wadsworth.

Egan, G. (2010) *The Skilled Helper: A Problem Management and Opportunity Development Approach to Helping*, 9th edn. London: Wadsworth.

Elbow, P. (1997) Freewriting and the problem: Wheat and tares. In J. M. Moxley and T. Taylor (eds), *Writing and Publishing for Academic Authors*, 2nd edn. London: Bowman and Littlefield.

Elliot, R., Greenburg, C. S. and Lieteaer, G. (2004) Research on experiential psychotherapies. In M. J. Lambert (ed.), *Bergin and Garfield's Handbook of Psychotherapy and Behavior Change*, 5th edn. Chichester: Wiley.

Feltham, C. (1995) *What Is Counselling?* London: Sage.

Feltham, C. (1996) Beyond denial, myth and superstition in the counselling profession. In R. Bayne, I. Horton and J. Bimrose (eds), *New Directions in Counselling*. London: Routledge.

Feltham, C. (2002) Starting in private practice. In J. Clark (ed.), *Freelance Counselling and Psychotherapy. Competition and Collaboration*. Hove: Brunner-Routledge.

Feltham C. and Dryden, W. (2006) *Brief Counselling. A Practical Integrative Approach*, 2nd edn. Maidenhead: Open University Press.

Frattaroli, J. (2006) Experimental disclosures and its moderators: a meta-analysis. *Psychological Bulletin* 132, 823–65.

Funder, D. (2007) *The Personality Puzzle*, 4th edn. London: W. W. Norton.

Furedi, F. (2003) *Therapy Culture: Cultivating Vulnerability in an Uncertain Age.* London Routledge.

Glover, B. and Shepherd, J. (1996) *The Runner's Handbook*, 3rd edn. Harmondsworth: Penguin.

Greetham, B. (2008) *How to Write Better Essays*, 2nd edn. London: Palgrave.

Grimmer, A. (2005) Personal therapy: researching a knotty problem. *Therapy Today* (September), 37–40.

Gunarata, B. (2002) *Mindfulness in Plain English.* Boston, MA: Wisdom Press.

Guy, J. D. (1987) *The Personal Life of the Psychotherapist.* New York: Wiley.

Hawkins, P. and Shohet, R. (2006) *Supervision in the Helping Professions*, 3rd edn. Oxford: Oxford University Press.

Hall, E., Hall, C., Stradling, P. and Young, D. (2006) *Guided Imagery. Creative Interventions in Counselling and Psychotherapy.* London: Sage.

Hill, C. E. and Lent, R. W. (2006) A narrative and meta-analytic review of helping skills training: Time to revive a dormant area of inquiry. *Psychotherapy: Theory, Research, Practice, Training* 43, 154–72.

Hodgson, S. (2008) *Brilliant Answers to Tough Interview Questions. Smart Answers to Whatever They Can Throw at You.* London: Pearson.

Hollon, S., Stewart, M. and Strunk, D. (2006) Enduring effects for Cognitive Behaviour Therapy in the treatment of depression and anxiety. *Annual Review of Psychology* 57, 285–315.

Horne, J. (2006) *Sleepfaring. A Journey through the Science of Sleep.* Oxford: Oxford University Press.

Horton, I. (2006a) Models of counselling and psychotherapy. In C. Feltham. and I. Horton (eds), *The Sage Handbook of Counselling and Psychotherapy*, 2nd edn. London: Sage.

Horton, I. (2006b) Integration. In C. Feltham and I. Horton (eds), *The Sage Handbook of Counselling and Psychotherapy*, 2nd edn. London: Sage.

Hubble, M. A., Duncan, B. L. and Miller, S. D. (eds) (1999) *The Heart and Soul of Change.* Washington, DC: APA Press.

Hunt, P. (1996) Marketing counselling courses. *Counselling* (August), 202–3.

Ivey, A., D'Andrea, M., Ivey, M. and Simek-Morgan, L. (2008) *Theories of Counselling and Psychotherapy: A Multicultural Perspective.* Harlow: Pearson Education.

Jenkins, P. (2007) *Counselling, Psychotherapy and the Law*, 2nd edn. London: Sage.

Jennings, L. and Skovholt, T. M. (1999) The cognitive, emotional and relational characteristics of master therapists. *Journal of Counseling Psychology* 46, 3–11.

Jinks, G. (2006) Specific strategies and techniques. In C. Feltham and I. Horton (eds), *The Sage Handbook of Counselling and Psychotherapy*, 2nd edn. London: Sage.

Jourard, S. (1964) *The Transparent Self.* London: D. Van Nostrand.

Jourard, S. (1971) *The Transparent Self*, rev. edn. London: Van Nostrand Reinhold.

Kagan, N. (1984) Interpersonal Process Recall: Basic methods and recent research. In D. Larsen (ed.), *Teaching Psychology Skills*. Monterey, CA: Brookes/Cole.

King, M., Semlyen, J., Killaspy, H., Nazareth, I. and Osborn, D. (2007) *A Systematic Review of Research on Counselling and Psychotherapy for Lesbian, Gay, Bisexual & Transgender People.* Lutterworth, Leicestershire: BACP.

Kwiatkowski, R. (1998) Counselling and psychotherapy: are they different and should we care? *Counselling Psychology Quarterly* 11, 5–14.

Lago, C. (2005) *Race, Culture and Counselling: The Ongoing Challenge.* Milton Keynes: Open University Press.

Lambert, M. J. (2004) *Bergin and Garfield's Handbook of Psychotherapy and Behavior Change*, 5th edn. Chichester: Wiley.

Lambert, M. J. and Ogles, B. M. (2004) The efficacy and effectiveness of psychotherapy. In M. J. Lambert (ed.), *Bergin and Garfield's Handbook of Psychotherapy and Behavior Change*, 5th edn. Chichester: Wiley.

Lazarus, A. A. (1978) 'Style' not 'systems'. *Psychotherapy: Theory, Research and Practice* 15, 359–61.

Lazarus, A. and Mayne, T. J. (1990) Relaxation: some limitations, side effects and proposed solutions. *Psychotherapy* 22, 261–6.

Leary, M. R., Tate, E. B., Adams, C. E., Allen, A. B. and Hancock, J. (2007) Self-comparison and reactions to unpleasant self-relevant events: the implications of treating oneself kindly. *Journal of Personality and Social Psychology* 92, 887–904.

Levin, P. (2004) *Write Great Essays: Reading and Essay Writing for Undergraduates and Taught Postgraduates.* Milton Keynes: Open University Press.

Linley, A. (2008) *Average to A+. Realising Strengths in Yourself and Others.* Coventry: CAPP Press.

Lyubomirsky, S., Sousa, L. and Dickerhoof, R. (2006) The cost and benefits of writing, talking and thinking about life's triumphs and defeats. *Journal of Personality and Social Psychology* 90, 692–708.

Macfarlane, A. (2007) Welcome to the strangers among us. *The Times Higher Education Supplement* (10 August), 14.

Mackenzie, A. and Hamilton, R. (2007) More than expected? Psychological outcomes from first-stage training in counselling. *Counselling Psychology Quarterly* 20, 229–45.

Mann, S. and Robinson, A. (2009) Boredom in the lecture theatre: an investigation into the contributors and outcomes of boredom amongst university students. *British Educational Research Journal* 35, 243–58.

Marsh, J. (1983) The boredom of study: A study of boredom. *Management Education and Development* 14, 120–35.

Martin, P. (2002) *Counting Sheep. The Science and Pleasures of Sleep and Dreams.* London: Flamingo.

Masson, J. (1989) *Against Therapy.* London: Collins.

McAdams, D. (1995) What do we know when we know a person? *Journal of Personality* 63, 365–96.

McLeod, J. (1997) Reading, writing and research. In I. Horton and V. Varma (eds), *The Needs of Counsellors and Psychotherapists.* London: Sage.

McLeod, J. (2003a) *An Introduction to Counselling*, 3rd edn. Buckingham: Open University Press.

McLeod, J. (2003b) *Doing Counselling Research*, 2nd edn. London: Sage.

McLeod, J. (2009) *An Introduction to Counselling*, 4th edn. Buckingham: Open University Press.

Miller, S., Hubble, M. and Duncan, B. (2008) Supershrinks. *Therapy Today* (April), 4–9.

Morrall, P. (2008) *The Trouble with Therapy: Sociology and Psychotherapy.* Milton Keynes: Open University Press.

Murray, R. (1997) *Ethical Humanities in Health Care: A Practical Approach through Medical Humanities.* Cheltenham: Nelson Thornes.

Murray, R. (1998) Communicating about ethical dilemmas: a medical humanities approach. In R. Bayne, P. Nicolson and I. Horton (eds), *Counselling and Communication Skills for Medical and Health Practitioners.* Oxford: Blackwell.

Nacif, A. P. (2004) Living with a trainee counsellor. *Counselling and Psychotherapy Journal* (March), 40–1.

Neff, K. D. and Vonk, R. (2008) Self-compassion versus global self-esteem: two different ways of relating to oneself. *Journal of Personality* 77, 23–50.

Nicklin, J. M. and Roch, S. G. (2009) Letters of recommendation: controversy and consensus from expert perspectives. *International Journal of Selection and Assessment* 17, 76–91.

Nicolson, P., Bayne, R. and Owen, J. (2006) *Applied Psychology for Social Workers*, 3rd edn. Basingstoke: Palgrave Macmillan.

Norcross, J. (2005) The psychotherapist's own psychotherapy: educating and developing psychologists. *American Psychologist* 60, 840–50.

Norcross, J. C. and Guy, J. D. (2007) *Leaving It at the Office. A Guide to Psychotherapists' Self-Care.* London: The Guilford Press.

O'Brien, M. and Houston, G. (2000) *Integrative Therapy – A Practitioner's Guide.* London: Sage.

Ogunfowora, B. and Drapeau, M. (2008) A study of the relationships between personality traits and theoretical orientation preferences. *Counselling and Psychotherapy Research* 8, 151–9.

Oleson, K. C. and Arkin, R. M. (2006) Reviewing and evaluating a research article. In F. T. L. Leong and J. T. Austin (eds), *The Psychology Research Handbook,* 2nd edn. London: Sage.

Patrick, E. (2003) Values? Now where did I put them? *Counselling and Psychotherapy Journal* (August), 30–1.

Payne, R. (2000) *Relaxation Techniques: A Practical Handbook for the Health Care Professional.* London: Churchill Livingstone.

Persaud, R. (1997) *Staying Sane: How to Make Your Mind Work for You.* London: Metro Brooks.

Provost, J. A. (1993) *A Casebook: Applications of the Myers–Briggs Type Indicator in Counseling,* 2nd edn. Gainesville, FL: Center for Applications of Psychological Type.

Radford, J. K. R. (2003) The professional academic. In R. Bayne and I. Horton (eds), *Applied Psychology. Current Issues and New Directions.* London: Sage.

Rainer, T. (1978) *The New Diary.* New York: St Martin's Press.

Rakos, R. (1991) *Assertive Behaviour: Theory, Research and Training.* London: Routledge.

Ridley, C. (2005) *Overcoming Unintentional Racism in Counselling and Therapy.* London: Sage.

Robson, C. (2002) *Real World Research. A Resource for Social Scientists and Practitioner-Researchers,* 2nd edn. Oxford: Blackwell.

Rodenburg, P. (2007) *Presence.* London: Penguin.

Rogers, C. R. (1961) *On Becoming a Person.* London: Constable.

Rogers, J. (2008) *Coaching Skills: A Handbook,* 2nd edn. Milton Keynes: Open University Press.

Rosenthal, T. (1993) To soothe the savage breast. *Behaviour Research and Therapy* 31, 439–62.

Russell, J. (1993) *Out of Bounds: Sexual Exploitation in Counselling and Therapy.* London: Sage.

Russell, J. (1996) Sexual exploitation in counselling. In R. Bayne, I. Horton and J. Bimrose (eds), *New Directions in Counselling.* London: Routledge.

Schenck, C. H. (2007) *Sleep. A Groundbreaking Guide to the Mysteries, the Problems, and the Solutions.* New York: Avery.

Schinkel, S. van Dierendonck, D. and Anderson, N. (2004) The impact of selection encounters on applicants: An experimental study into feedback effects after a negative selection decision. *International Journal of Selection and Assessment* 12, 197–205.

Schlosberg, S. and Neporent, L. (2005) *Fitness for Dummies,* 3rd edn. Chichester: Wiley.

Scragg, P., Bor, R. and Watts, M. (1999) The influence of personality and theoretical models on applicants to a counselling course: A preliminary study. *Counselling Psychology Quarterly* 12, 263–70.

Segal, Z., Williams, J. and Teasdale, J. (2002) *Mindfulness-Based Cognitive Therapy for Depression.* London: Guilford Press.

Seligman, M. E. P. (2002) *Authentic Happiness: Using the Science of Positive Psychology to Realise Your Potential for Lasting Fulfilment.* London: Nicholas Brealey.

Simon, S. B., Howe, L. W. and Kirschenbaum, H. (1995) *Values Clarification,* rev. edn. London: Little, Brown & Company.

Singer, J. A. (2005) *Personality and Psychotherapy. Treating the Whole Person.* London: The Guilford Press.

Skovholt, T. and Ronnestad, M. (1995) *The Evolving Professional Self.* Chichester: Wiley.

Spencer, L. (2006) Tutors' stories of personal development training – attempting to maximise the learning potential. *Counselling and Psychotherapy Research* 6, 108–14.

Spinelli, E. and Marshall, S. (eds) (2001) *Embodied Theories.* London: Continuum.

Storr, A. (1990) *The Art of Psychotherapy,* 2nd edn. London: Heinemann/ Secker and Warburg.

Sugarman, L. (2001) *Life-span Development: Frameworks, Accounts and Strategies.* London: Routledge.

Sussman, M. (1992) *A Curious Calling: Unconscious Motivation for Practising Psychotherapy.* New York: Jason Aronson.

Talmon, M. (1990) *Single-Session Therapy.* San-Francisco: Jossey-Bass.

Taylor, S. E. (2009) *Health Psychology,* 7th edn. London: McGraw-Hill.

Templer, D. I. (1971) Analyzing the psychotherapist. *Mental Hygiene* 55, 234–6.

Ten Have, P. (2007) *Doing Conversation Analysis,* 2nd edn. London: Sage.

Thorne, B. (1992) Psychotherapy and counselling: the quest for differences. *Counselling* 3 (4), 244–8.

Tieger, P. D. and Barron-Tieger, B. (2000) *Just Your Type: the Relationship You've Always Wanted Using the Secrets of Personality Type.* London: Little, Brown.

Tieger, P. D. and Barron-Tieger, B. (2007) *Do What You Are. Discover the Perfect Career for You through the Secrets of Personality Type,* 4th edn. London: Little Brown.

Tompkins, P., Sullivan, W. and Lawley, J. (2005) Tangled spaghetti in my head. *Therapy Today* (October), 32–6.

Truell, R. (2001) The stresses of learning counselling: six recent graduates comment on their personal experience of learning counselling and what can be done to reduce associated harm. *Counselling Psychology Quarterly* 14, 67–89.

Varlami, E. and Bayne, R. (2007) Psychological type and counselling psychology trainees' choice of counselling orientations. *Counselling Psychology Quarterly* 20, 361–73.

Wade, C. and Tavris, C. (1993) *Psychology*, 3rd edn. London: Prentice Hall.

Waines, A. (2004) *The Self-Esteem Journal: Using a Journal to Build Self-Esteem.* London: Sheldon.

Weiten, W. (2007) *Psychology Themes and Variations*, 7th edn. London: Thomson.

Wessely, S. (2001) Randomised controlled trials: the gold standard. In C. Mace, S. Moorey and B. Roberts (eds), *Evidence in the Psychological Therapies.* Hove: Brunner-Routledge.

Whalley, S. and Jackson, L. (2008) *Zest: Running Made Easy*, rev. edn. London: Robson Books.

Wheen, F. (2004) *How Mumbo-Jumbo Conquered the World.* London: Harper Perennial.

Wilkins, P. (1997) *Personal and Professional Development for Counsellors.* London: Sage.

Williams, E. and Scott, M. (2006) Anger control. In C. Feltham and I. Horton (eds), *The Sage Handbook of Counselling and Psychotherapy*, 2nd edn. London: Sage.

Worden, J. W. (2008) *Grief Counselling and Grief Therapy: A Handbook for the Mental Health Practitioner.* New York: Springer.

Wortman, C. and Silver, R. (1989) The myths of coping with loss. *Journal of Consulting and Clinical Psychology* 57(3), 349–57.

Wright, J. K. (2005) Writing therapy in brief workplace counselling. *Counselling and Psychotherapy Research* 5, 111–19.

Yalom, I. D. (1989) *Love's Executioner and Other Tales of Psychotherapy.* Harmondsworth: Penguin.

Yalom, I. D. (2001) *The Gift of Therapy. Reflections on Being a Therapist.* London: Piatkus.

Name index

Subject index